VOODOO
NETWARE

TIPS & TRICKS WITH AN ATTITUDE

VOODOO NETWARE

TIPS & TRICKS WITH AN ATTITUDE

Emmett Dulaney

For Version 4.0

Ventana Press Voodoo™ Series

Voodoo NetWare: Tips & Tricks With an Attitude for Version 4.0
Copyright © 1993 by Emmett Dulaney
Ventana Press Voodoo™ Series

Library of Congress Cataloging-in-Publication Data
Dulaney, Emmett A.
    Voodoo NetWare : tips & tricks with an attitude / Emmett Dulaney.
  --1st ed.
     p. cm.
    Includes bibliographical references and index.
    ISBN 1-56604-077-9
    1. Operating systems (Computers) 2. NetWare (Computer file)
  I. Title.
  QA76.76.063D857   1993
  005.7'1369--dc20   93-24450
                                           CIP

Book design: Karen Wysocki
Cover Illustration: Lynn Tanaka, Lynn Tanaka Illustration
Cover design: Thea Tullose, Tullose Design; John Nedwidek, Sitzer:Spuria
Index Service: Stephen E. Bach
Editorial staff: Charles Hutchinson, Pam Richardson
Proofreaders: Eric Edstam, Jean Kaplan
Production staff: Cabell Smith, Marcia Webb, Karen Wysocki
Technical review: Barbara R. Hume, Network Technical Services

First Edition 9 8 7 6 5 4 3 2 1
Printed in the United States of America

Ventana Press, Inc.
P.O. Box 2468
Chapel Hill, NC 27515
919/942-0220
FAX 919/942-1140

Limits of Liability and Disclaimer of Warranty

Trademarks

COLOPHON

Voodoo NetWare was produced on a Macintosh LC, using Aldus PageMaker 4.2. Body text is set in Digital Typeface Corporation (DTC) Galliard Roman. Tip and trap names, running heads and subheads are DTC Optimum Bold. Chapter heads are Tribeca and folios are set in DTC Dom Casual. Screen shots were taken with Collage software and cover art was produced on a Macintosh Quadra 800 using QuarkXPress 3.11 and Adobe Illustrator 5.

About the Author

Emmett Dulaney is the author of several computer books, including *NetWare Solutions and Shortcuts* (M&T Publishing) and *UNIX Unleashed* (Sams). He is also an associate professor of Continuing Education at Indiana/Purdue University of Fort Wayne, IN, and a senior support representative for BI, Inc.

Acknowledgments

It is such an injustice to so many to put only one name on the cover of a book. In reality, a book is a group effort involving dozens of unsung individuals. The finished product you hold in your hands would not be the same were it not for the unique contributions of each.

I would like to thank Elizabeth and Joe Woodman, Pam Richardson, and the crew at Ventana Press for their assistance and guidance. They took an active part in the process from start to finish.

Thanks also are due Barbara Hume and Chuck Hutchinson, technical editor and editor, respectively. Their insight and fine-tuning were helpful.

Renae McIntyre tirelessly worked on the companion disk, and deserves a pat on the back for diligence. Thanks also are due Matt Wagner at Waterside Productions for his encouragement. And to anyone else not mentioned who may have contributed—a tip, trap or word of encouragement—your assistance is greatly appreciated.

TABLE OF CONTENTS

WHAT'S NEW IN NETWARE 4.0

Whereas previous NetWare versions have always been improvements on their predecessors—offering a better means of networking—NetWare 4.0 is a completely different product. Instead of being an improvement on versions 2.x and 3.x, it is a departure from their means of operations and a journey in a different direction.

To begin with, NetWare 4.0 is not intended for the smaller customer, and it will not be worth your while to upgrade a LAN consisting of one or two servers. Large networks with multiple servers are the intended users of this product—and the only ones who will truly benefit from the changes. Novell will continue to market the other versions of NetWare and has no plans at this time to discontinue any.

The biggest change in NetWare 4.0 is the replacement of bindery services with the NetWare Directory Service, or NDS. NDS is a global database, which is replicated and maintained on every server across the network. With this database, a user can access all servers with one login and not have to maintain an individual account on every server, as was done in the past.

Other changes include disk compression of files not accessed for a period of time, improved backup features, time synchronization across the network, and login scripts for groups—known as *profiles*. These changes will be discussed in limited detail here and in greater detail in chapters that pertain to their topics.

NETWARE DIRECTORY SERVICE

The bindery is dead; long live the NDS!

NetWare has used a flat file database since the early days to keep track of users, passwords and so on. This database was called the *bindery*, and it served its purpose well on the server where it resided. If a user on one server needed to access functions on another server, that user had to have an account in the bindery of the second server, complete with passwords, permissions and so on. Even though the servers were connected on the same LAN, they didn't share information about their binderies.

With 4.0, there is one database, a hierarchical tree that exists across the network and is distributed and replicated on every server. In this way, the user is recognized on every server, and the transition from server to server is seamless. Groups exist network-wide, and the replicas are updated on each server with synchronized regularity. Thus, if a new user is added, the administrator needs to add the user only once, and the new information will be added to each server on the network as synchronization takes place.

Every item on the network has now become an object. Objects include users, groups, servers and so on. Queues and printers also have become objects and thus can be accessed system-wide and not just by local users anymore.

There are two levels of objects: container and key. Container objects hold key objects or other containers (remember: *objects* is the new term for everything). Key, or leaf, objects are the lowest level and do not have other objects beneath them.

There are three types of container objects:

- Country (CN)

- Organization (O)

- Organizational Unit (OU)

There are many types of key, or leaf, objects, and a complete list follows:

Key Object	Description
Alias	A pointer to another location
Bindery	A previously created object that NDS cannot identify
Computer	A workstation, printer, etc.
Directory Map	A directory on a volume
Group	A subset of selected users
Server	A server on the LAN
Organizational Role	A position that different people can fill
Print Server	A workstation to handle print requests

Key Object	Description
Printer	A physical printer
Profile	A login script for a special group
Print Queue	A memory area for print requests to wait for a printer
User	Anyone who can log into the network
Unknown	An NDS object that is corrupted
Volume	A hard drive area partitioned for NetWare files

Most leaf objects have common names; for example, a user's common name can be his or her login name. Container objects, on the other hand, do not have common names and are referred to by Organizational Unit name or Organization or Country name.

An object's complete name is its common name followed by a period, then the name of the container object, a period and so on, all the way up through the directory tree. For example, the following complete name refers to user EDULANEY who works in the SUPPORT division of OPERATIONS for the organization BI:

```
CN=EDULANEY.OU=SUPPORT.OU=OPERATIONS.O=BI US
```

Even when you refer to objects located in the same container object, you often must designate the name type (CN, OU or O) of the object.

Bindery emulation is included with this version of NetWare to let a NetWare 4.0 server talk to earlier version servers by emulating their flat structure database.

DISK COMPRESSION

The disk compression feature that comes with NetWare 4.0 is actually a misnomer. As opposed to compressing the entire disk (as MS-DOS DBLSPACE and Stac Electronic's Stacker do), NetWare compresses individual files. In compressing the files, the free disk space increases —by an average of about 63 percent—and that is where the savings come in.

The compression takes place on files that have not been accessed for a number of days and occurs at off hours so that server processing is not slowed down any more than necessary. By default, files not accessed in six days are compressed between midnight and six a.m. You can change these parameters as needed and set an individual file's attributes to prevent it from ever being compressed. Compression is extremely important with database files and other sizable files that you need to access as quickly as possible and not be delayed by the time it would take to decompress them before reading.

BACKUP IMPROVEMENTS

You now can create unattended backups, and NetWare 4.0 supports only tape media for backup. No longer do you whittle away an entire Saturday backing up the server to 5.25-inch DS/DD disks.

Tape sizes supported are 1/4 inch, 4mm and 8mm. And now you can perform a backup that spans more than one tape, providing the medium you use is compliant.

TIME SYNCHRONIZATION

Time synchronization allows all servers in the NDS to report the same time. When you install NetWare 4.0, you are asked whether you want to designate the server as a single reference, primary, reference or secondary time server.

Single reference means that this server provides its time to secondary servers and to workstations attached. The administrator must maintain the time on the server.

Primary servers synchronize their time with at least one other primary or reference server and provide that time to secondary servers and attached workstations. If a primary server goes down, a secondary server can get the time from another primary.

Reference servers provide time to other servers only. They provide a reference and nothing more.

Secondary time servers provide time to workstations that they receive from a primary server.

PROFILES

Profiles are login scripts that exist for groups instead of users. Any subset of users can become a group that the system administrator sets up. These groups can be based on location, department, job duties and so on. When the user logs in, the script for the group will run.

OTHER FEATURES

Burst Mode protocol is now supported in NetWare 4.0. Instead of using the one-request/one-response protocol of earlier versions, now the network sends requests in packets, resulting in reduced network traffic and a drop in the number of required read and write operations.

A Directory Entry Table (DET) and File Allocation Table (FAT) contain address information about where data can be retrieved from. Duplicate copies of DET and FAT are stored elsewhere on the disk. Each time the server is booted, a consistency check is performed on all four files to verify that their corresponding files are identical.

Memory management has been redesigned to increase efficiency. NetWare 3.11 had five different memory pools that served different purposes. Occasionally, after continuous operation, one ran out of memory for an application and was unable to allocate from another pool. NetWare 4.0 uses one pool from which all resources can pull.

Block suballocation divides disk blocks among several files to make better use of server disk space.

Data migration is available to transfer inactive data to offline storage mediums such as disk, tape and CD-ROM, while NetWare 4.0 still sees the data as residing on the drive. If the file is referenced, NetWare moves it back onto the disk.

Now you also can adapt messages to multiple languages. The operating system supports French, Italian, German and Spanish.

NetWare print services have been created for this version. Now the print server, print queue and printer are viewed as individual objects, as opposed to the way they were under bindery operations. You now can create and modify them in any order, and a user can send print jobs directly to a printer by specifying the printer name and not the queue.

Online documentation has been provided via a CD-ROM disk that holds the entire manual.

NEW SERVER UTILITIES

Several new server utilities were added to the operating system to increase flexibility. These include the following:

- *Abort remirror.* Stops the remirroring of a logical disk partition.

- *Keyb.* Changes the nationality or language of the server keyboard.

- *Language.* Sets the server to use specific message files for different languages.

- *List devices.* Shows device information on the server.

- *Magazine.* Confirms fulfillment of magazine requests.

- *Media.* Confirms fulfillment of media requests.

- *Mirror status.* Displays all mirrored logical partitions.

- *Remirror partition.* Starts remirroring of logical disk partitions.

- *Scan for new devices.* Checks for disk hardware added since the last boot of the server.

NEW NLMs

Ten new NetWare Loadable Modules were added:

- *CDROM.* Allows the server to use a read-only volume.

- *DOMAIN.* Creates a protected OS domain.

- *DSREPAIR.* Acts as Directory Service repair utility and re-placement for BINDFIX.

- *NPRINTER.* Allows any server's printer to become a network printer.

- *NWSNUT.* Acts as NLM Utility User Interface.

- *RPL.* Allows you to boot IBM-compatible PCs remotely.

- *RTDM.* Creates real-time data migration.

- *SBACKUP.* Completes all backup requests from anywhere on the network.

- *SERVMAN.* Changes SET parameters in .NCF files.

- *TIMESYNC.* Controls time synchronization on servers that are running NDS.

NEW UTILITIES

Six new utilities that you can run from workstations were included with NetWare 4.0. They are as follows:

- *AUDITCON.* Tracks usage of network resources.

- *CX.* Changes the current context.

- *MENU.* Drastically changed from previous versions, this utility allows you to create simplified operating environments for users.

■ *NLIST.* Lists the information about files, directories, users, groups, volumes, servers, queues, objects and their properties.

■ *NPRINTER.* Creates a network printer.

■ *UIMPORT.* Imports an ASCII file into the NDS.

NEW MENUS

Following are the four new menus in NetWare 4.0:

■ *NETADMIN.* Governs the creation and management of objects.

■ *NETUSER.* Sets up print jobs and changes configurations.

■ *PARTMGR.* Manages the partition.

■ *PSETUP.* Sets up printers and utilities.

OS/2

All utilities that exist in the DOS world also exist in the OS/2 realm, with the exception of the following, which do not exist on the OS/2 version of NetWare: COLORPAL, FILER, NETADMIN, PARTMGR, RENDIR and WSUPDATE.

PRICE

As with all versions of NetWare, pricing is based on the number of users on the network. This number is the number of workstations that *can* access that network, not the number that concurrently *do*. So, if you have ten workstations, but only three people work on each shift, you still must have a 10-user package to be legal.

The following prices are current at the time of this printing and are offered only as reference. For more information, contact Novell, Inc. at 122 East 1700 South, Provo, UT 84606 or call them at (800) 453-1267.

Package	Cost
5-user system	$1,395
10-user	$3,195
25-user	$4,695
50-user	$6,295
100-user	$8,795
200-user	$15,695
500-user	$26,395
1000-user	$47,995

MOVING ON

In this preface, I discussed the new features available in NetWare 4.0 and stressed that the operating system is not intended for small LANs. I now must assume that you fall into the category of those who will benefit from the features provided, and we can continue onward.

The Introduction and Chapter 1, "Hardware Secrets," follow. In the first chapter, I will discuss what is required in terms of hardware before moving into peculiarities of the operating system itself.

INTRODUCTION

NetWare is a voodoo subject if ever there was one. Novell's own documentation stretches from here to the moon, seminars and workshops could take all your time, and even the best third-party consultants and dealers are often confounded by its strange ways. In brief, even the most seasoned NetWare administrator—not to mention the un-anointed—is often reduced to waving chicken bones and shouting encomiums when troubleshooting many of the complex hardware and software problems surrounding NetWare.

Voodoo NetWare can provide some help. While most books discuss an operating system painstaking detail by painstaking detail, *Voodoo NetWare* takes a different approach—bringing out the key points of NetWare by offering practical gems of advice, organized in a non-linear format by subject area.

With the release of 4.0, NetWare created two routes to accomplish many of the same tasks: through the command line and through menu choices. Chapter 2, "Menu Magic," concentrates on the menus and introduces you to the tricks they provide. Throughout the rest of the book, however, you'll notice a strong leaning toward the command-line approach. The reasoning behind this is simple: menus are straightforward and involve little more than moving the cursor and pressing the Enter key. Anyone who knows which menus exist can perform operations with little training.

The command line is not so straightforward. There are many tricks and pitfalls to share. Knowledge of these command-line tricks saves you tremendous amounts of time and gives you more specific control of the operating system.

Chapters in *Voodoo NetWare* are broken into logical content, and the tips and traps are intended to give you a clearer understanding of the NetWare 4.0 operating system. Where shortcuts are available, you'll find a tip, and where pitfalls await the unsuspecting, you'll find a trap.

Because NetWare is an advanced operating system, I must assume that you are familiar with networking and the NetWare environment. Whether you are currently using version 4.0 or considering the upgrade, you will find this book useful in helping you get the most out of your software. There are no sections, however, on programming NLMs; *Voodoo NetWare* is an operating system book, not a programming book.

WHAT'S INSIDE

Here's a quick preview of *Voodoo NetWare*, to help you find the areas of immediate interest to you.

Preface: What's New in NetWare 4.0

If you've not already upgraded to 4.0, you're probably wondering if it's for you. Instead of being an upgrade to existing versions of the operating system, this version is a radical departure from it. This preface will outline the differences and help you determine whether or not you should upgrade.

Chapter 1: Hardware Secrets

What does NetWare 4.0 require in terms of server and memory? Is it better to go with more RAM or a faster processor? What about topologies and network cards? You'll find the answers to these puzzling quandaries in this chapter.

Chapter 2: Menu Magic

One of NetWare's strong points has always been the menus, which allow you to see quickly what is happening across the network. Some of the menus that existed in previous versions are gone, and new menus take their places. This chapter outlines those menus, with practical advice on how to use them for maximum efficiency.

Chapter 3: Command-line Sorcery

All those options and parameters: which are needed and which can't you avoid no matter how hard you try? Read this chapter to learn what you need to know to handle networking from the dreaded command line.

Chapter 4: File Wizardry

Of primary importance to system administrators, this chapter discusses login scripts, backups and security, to name just a few topics.

Chapter 5: Directory & File Incantations

The directory tree is the structure that holds all files on the server. After you learn the workings of the tree, you will also go over object and property rights, attributes and utilities that let you move, rename and modify.

Chapter 6: Printer Enchantment

One of the most difficult things about computing, on a network or not, is getting text to print on a printer and making certain that all appears as it should. This chapter will help you do just that.

Chapter 7: Workstation Wonders

In terms of quantity, workstations outnumber any other network component. This chapter covers differences in MS-DOS and DR DOS as well as diskless workstations and troubleshooting.

Chapter 8: Windows Marvels

More and more, the Microsoft Windows software is working its way into the world of computing and onto workstations connected to NetWare networks. This chapter will help you link NetWare and Windows into a potent mixture.

Chapter 9: Miscellaneous Alchemy

This chapter is a mixed assortment of information relating to groups, trustees and server utilities.

Chapter 10: Troubleshooting

When all else fails, here is the place to turn. General troubleshooting is covered in the first half of the chapter, and specific responses to error messages fill the second half.

Appendices

The appendices offer a glossary of terms, instructions for upgrading an existing NetWare network to version 4.0 and a list of the most often configured options contained in .NCF files.

HOW TO USE THIS BOOK

To get the most out of this book, you need to be familiar with Net-Ware networks and either be running version 4.0 or giving it some serious thought.

In all the examples shown, unless otherwise specified, I am assuming you have workstations with hard drives. Therefore C: stands for the first local drive, and F: is the first drive of the network.

You can enter all command-line entries in upper- or lowercase; there is no discretion in NetWare. In this book, the command appears in all uppercase.

USE THE INDEX

The index at the back of this book is the quickest means available to find the specific topic you're looking for. While chapters have been categorized, a command or option may span two topics. The only way to know for sure is to use the index.

YOUR FAVORITE TRICK

If you use NetWare 4.0 and have a favorite trick that is not covered in this book, send it to Ventana or to me, and we'll try to get it in the next edition. If we include your trick, the next edition is yours free; thus, be sure to include your name and address.

You can contact Ventana Press, P.O. Box 2468, Chapel Hill, NC 27515, telephone (919) 942-0220 or fax (919) 942-1140. Or write to me at P.O. Box 353, Muncie, IN 47308.

—Emmett Dulaney

Chapter 1
HARDWARE SECRETS

Before Netware 4.0 can be up and running, a hardware platform must be in place for it to operate on. You must have a server, network cards and enough cable to link everything together. The software comes into play only when the hardware is in place. Thus, before I begin the discussion of NetWare in subsequent chapters, I will first review the basics of hardware selection, requirements and connection. If you already have the hardware in place, I still recommend you skim the section on servers to be certain you're meeting the requirements for an efficient operation.

If the operating system is the brains of the network, then the hardware is the physical body. Often we concentrate on the brain and try to get it to perform in the way we would like for it to, without taking into account the physical structure that provides its confines. With a good body, or physical structure, it is easier to get NetWare 4.0 to perform at peak capacity and ensure that it will continue to do so for long durations of time.

Servers, network cards and cables provide the skeletal structure that I will discuss in this chapter. I'll try to provide enough detail to prevent these elements from becoming ailments. I'll discuss hardware in following chapters only in so much as it pertains to the topic—such as printers in the printing chapter—but only in this chapter do I discuss the server, network cards and cabling. Some of the information will be basic, pertaining to all networks, while other portions will be specific only to NetWare 4.0. Now it's time to begin.

SERVER CRITERIA

You should check out the requirements and tips in this section if you are purchasing a new server or upgrading your present one to accommodate NetWare 4.0. If you already have 4.0 up and running with no difficulties, I still suggest that you skim this section before you go to the next chapter.

 Think speed when you select your server. When you select a file server, bear in mind that the speed at which it operates will dictate the speed at which workstations linked to it can complete their server-access functions. If you spend a fortune purchasing Pentium workstations and expect them to perform network functions more quickly when accessing a 386 file server than their 286 counterparts did, then you are sadly mistaken. The most crucial component of the network is the file server, and it should be of superior quality to any workstations attached to it.

 Following are five items you should contemplate when considering the purchase of a new server:

- *Modular CPU cards.* These cards give you the opportunity to upgrade the server's processor in the future, without needing to replace the entire motherboard.

■ *Fault tolerance features.* Currently, the most popular option is the Redundant Array of Inexpensive Disks, or RAID, technology. This feature allows the server to function even when error conditions are present.

■ *RAM capacity.* Find out the maximum amount of RAM the machine is capable of supporting. It is not uncommon to find servers now able to support 300mb of RAM. While that amount may seem a large number today, there is no telling what will be considered a suitable number tomorrow. Not that long ago, 64k seemed like sufficient RAM on home computers, and now you are hard-pressed to find many programs that can operate within that confine.

■ *Support.* What type of support is available and what is the maximum response time? Is the support on-site, or does it require removing the server? If the server cannot be repaired in a timely fashion, is a replacement server offered? The rub to always remember is that when the server is down, so are the workstations that must access it; thus, support becomes one very big issue.

■ *Price.* You can spend as little or as much as you want on a server. You can convert a regular PC to a file server at the low end of the spectrum, or you can use a stand-alone tower at the high end. Everyone must come to his or her own ideal position on the server that works based on need and resources available.

Consider upgrading your present server. To upgrade the performance of your server, you need not always purchase a new one. Two valid options are to upgrade the server's processor or add more RAM.

Avoid RAM cram. Increasing the amount of RAM allows NetWare to increase the amount of memory cache. The more memory that is stored in the cache, the less time NetWare has to spend accessing the drive, thus the quicker the access/response time.

Calculate how much RAM you need. NetWare 4.0 requires a minimum of a 386 processor with 8mb of RAM. Novell recommends using the following five-step formula for determining the amount of RAM necessary at an installation:

1. Start with 5.5mb.

2. Add 2mb if you're going to use a print server on this server.

3. Add 2mb if you're going to use loaded modules such as STREAMS.NLM or BTRIEVE.NLM.

4. Multiply the hard drive size by .008 and add the result to the existing amount.

5. Add between 1mb and 4mb for additional cache memory. The result is the ideal RAM size for your installation.

General Rule: Buy the fastest server with the largest SCSI hard disk you can afford, with a minimum of 8 to 16mb RAM. Novell's recommendation is that the minimum amount of RAM required to run NetWare 4.0 is 8mb. I recommend 16mb as the minimum amount of RAM required to run 4.0, but don't be afraid to bump that number up to 32mb.

The more RAM present, the more memory available for disk caching, and the faster the server is going to operate. Given a limited budget and the options of choosing between a faster motherboard or more RAM, go with more RAM every time.

Consider access speed. One of the most important criteria in server selection should be the access speed of the hard drive. A slower drive can constitute one of the largest slowdowns on the network, whereas a quick drive can be one of its most important assets.

Think of the hard drive size. The absolute minimum hard drive size allowed is 30mb; however, you should not configure a file server utilizing a minimum hard drive. This area is one where larger can only mean better. The more room available for storing files, the more effective the file server will be. The maximum space recognized by the operating system is 32tb.

The minimum hard drive size allowed for an OS/2 installation jumps to 120mb. If you intend to install the help documentation that is included on the CD-ROM, then add another 40mb to the hard drive size, whether you are using a DOS-based operating system or OS/2.

Subtract space without the manual. If you're not going to install the electronic text on the server but you plan to read it directly from the CD-ROM, the 40mb requirement drops to 1mb of disk space on the server.

Look at block size. A *block* is the size of the smallest amount of hard disk space that can be allocated at one time by a NetWare volume. To minimize requirements that are placed on RAM, watch the hard drive block size, which is dependent on the size of the volume in the following manner:

Volume Size	Block Size
0 to 32mb	4k
32 to 150mb	8k
150 to 500mb	16k
500 to 2000mb	32k
2000+mb	64k

Block suballocation then divides partially used blocks into 512-byte suballocation units, which share the block with leftover fragments of other files. If the server block size computes to 8k and you have a 9k file, it will occupy one 8k block plus 2 suballocation units—leaving 7mb of the second block available for use by another file.

Fault tolerance should be an essential. Fault tolerance is the server's capability to keep working, even though it may have received some type of error. NetWare recognizes many different types of fault tolerance that are available in hardware and software. You should entertain them all as possibilities in your networking environment, if not necessities.

The software itself is designed to be fault tolerant (see subsequent chapters), but in addition to this tolerance, you also can perform such operations as mirroring or duplexing of the hard drive. Thus, if the hard drive fails, operations switch to the mirrored drive until the problems are corrected.

Think beyond the server. When you're purchasing or configuring a server, note that in addition to the server, you will also need one network board and sufficient cabling to install it as a file server. I discuss these requirements in subsequent sections of this chapter.

NETWORK CARDS

Network Interface Cards, or NICs, go between the server or workstation and the cable connecting the network together. Cards slip into slots in the CPUs and allow the server and workstations to communicate with each other. Every packet of data that is sent from a workstation is received by the server. Every packet that is sent by the server, in turn, is received by the workstation's card. The card then determines whether the packet is intended for this particular workstation. If so, it is processed. On the other hand, if the packet is not intended for this workstation, it is then overlooked and left for processing by another workstation.

Although network cards do not represent the most expensive element of the network, they do represent one of the most recurring purchases. Each time you add another workstation to an existing network, you must purchase another NIC card. The tips and tricks in this section relate to the too-often-overlooked card.

Three ways NIC cards work. Network cards work in three key, but different, ways to move the information they contain between the workstation's RAM and the network cable. The first type utilizes direct memory access, or DMA. This type was designed for use in early PCs and operates with a slow timing signal. When they're placed in fast workstations, the DMA cards still run at the same slow rate and thus are not used as frequently in newer installations.

The second type of card uses shared memory to access the workstation's memory directly and process it with a zero-wait state. These cards work well when properly configured, but often there can be conflicts with other components inside the workstation.

The third card type uses programmed I/O to control only a shared block of memory rather than the entire workstation's memory. The contents of the block are quickly shifted in and out as commands are found and executed. The majority of NetWare-based cards utilize some type of programmed I/O.

Diskless stations require different cards. For diskless workstations, you will need cards that support remote-boot ROM. ROM gives the workstation the capability to download the DOS files it needs to boot up when the user first turns on the power.

Internal collisions can occur. Interrupts, or IRQs, are unique numbers assigned to each component within a CPU, be it a workstation or server. Every NIC card comes with a default interrupt number, and you must be careful that another board within the workstation or server is not utilizing the same interrupt number.

On the plus side, most network cards work properly when they're configured with the defaults recommended by the manufacturer. If they do not work properly, you can almost always use an alternative configuration outlined in the short card description provided by the manufacturer.

One of the most common interrupt conflicts is when the NIC card and an internal modem are set to the same IRQ. If such is the case, the workstation will lose connection to the server after a user finishes using the modem. The easiest solution, given this scenario, is always to change the IRQ on the modem as opposed to changing it on the NIC card.

Laptop cards. NIC cards, by nature of design, virtually always use one of the workstation's expansion slots—something that many laptop computers, because of their reduced size, do not come with. Many vendors offer external cards that connect to the laptop's parallel port and function in the same way but are usually slower.

Meet the MAC. Media Access Control, or MAC, is the set of rules that LANs utilize to avoid data collisions. Two sets of rules govern the way MAC works: one is the type used in token ring, and the other is Carrier Sense Multiple Access, or CSMA. You can mix and match different vendors and flavors of network cards on the same network, providing all the cards use the same MAC protocol.

TOPOLOGY

No matter what terminology you utilize, really only two physical topologies are ever used in networking NetWare workstations: the *star* and the *daisy chain*. *Bus* topology refers to a derivative of the daisy chain wherein all workstations receive a message at the same time. Figure 1-1 shows an example of the star topology.

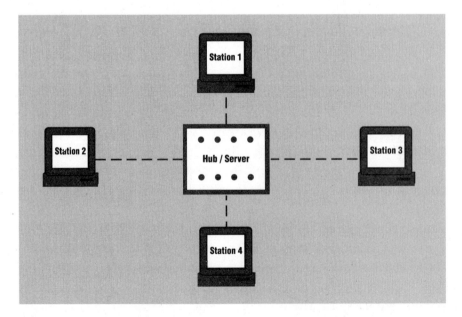

Figure 1-1: The star topology.

Each workstation has a direct connection to a hub, or it connects directly to the server. If you have a problem with the connection to one workstation, the problem stays isolated there.

Figure 1-2 illustrates the daisy chain topology.

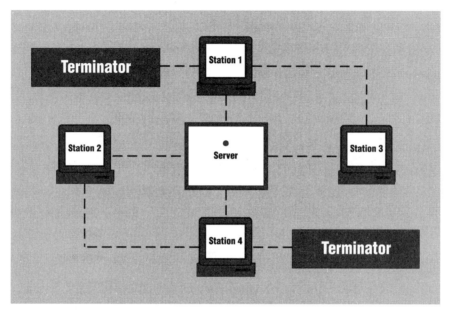

Figure 1-2: The daisy chain topology.

All workstations are connected to the cable via T-connections. One end of the "T" is carrying information from the server; whether or not the cabling came from another workstation between this one and the server is inconsequential. The cable coming from the other end of the "T" goes to workstations down the line from this one. At each end of the network, a terminator must signal the end of the line.

Pay careful attention to every connection. Because all the workstations share the same line, if there is a problem at one workstation, it affects all workstations. A cabling problem or a bad "T" connector can effectively bring the network to a standstill.

Daisy chain topology uses far less cable than star topology. Additionally, it does not require room for a wiring hub because it connects directly to the server.

Don't save money and create problems. If you use a daisy chain, never attempt to save money by buying cheaper "T" connectors or terminators. Because the network is only as strong as its weakest link, this link is one you want to pay particular attention to. Stay as far way from cheap twist-on connectors as possible—they are notorious for coming loose.

In addition to the two types of physical topologies, there are several logical topologies, including Ethernet, token ring and ARCnet.

Ethernet is the most popular. Thin Ethernet, or thinnet, is one of the most common installations in practice today. If you use the daisy chain topology, the overall cable length supported by this type of installation cannot exceed 1,000 feet.

Additional restrictions are that you can have up to 5 different "trunks" with a maximum of 100 workstations tied to each trunk. Both ends of the cable must be terminated with 50 ohm terminators, and one of the terminators must be grounded.

Standard Ethernet. Standard Ethernet uses thicker cable than that used by Thin Ethernet. Instead of connecting the cable directly to the back of each workstation via a "T" connector, you run the cable through transceivers, which then connect to the back of the workstations in the same manner.

The cable is thicker and harder to manage in terms of trying to conceal and make it as aesthetically appealing as possible, but it does support longer connections. An overall cable length of 1,500 feet is possible using Standard, instead of Thin, Ethernet.

Additional restrictions are that you can have up to 5 different "trunks" with a maximum of 100 workstations on each trunk. The maximum distance between transceivers is 8 feet, and the maximum length of a transceiver cable is 165 feet. Both ends of the cable are terminated with type "N" terminators, and one end is grounded.

10BaseT is gaining ground. 10BaseT is presently being touted by many network users as the new favorite way to cable a network. Essentially, this cabling system is the same as Ethernet, only now it is running on twisted pair wiring and in the star topology. Although the major advantage of 10BaseT is that it removes the one-bad-workstation-wrecking-the-whole-network problem, it does add additional components to the system, such as wiring hubs that require AC power.

Token ring has always been the networking method IBM has touted. If you use a star topology, shielded wires connect each workstation to hubs that are referred to as Multistation Access Units, or MAUs. The difference between token ring and Ethernet is that each workstation's network card listens to what is being transmitted across the network and waits until nothing is going on. When all is calm, the network transmits its data and awaits a response. This method is much like taking a subway token and waiting for the train to come into the station, hence the name.

Fiber optic cable has further limitations. Although typically it uses shielded twisted pair, token ring also can utilize fiber optic cable. One major drawback is that the maximum cable length between the hub and the workstation cannot exceed 150 feet.

Twisted pair can be used with ARCnet. Traditionally ARCnet uses coaxial cable in a star topology, but it also can use unshielded twisted pair. The maximum cable length is 2,000 feet, which makes it a good choice for large installations.

High-Impedance ARCnet. A version of ARCnet known as High-Impedance ARCnet is available. It utilizes daisy chain topology and can have cable lengths up to 20,000 feet.

CABLING

The type of cabling that you use must be based on the type of network interface cards and topology in the network. The topology and interface cards you use, on the other hand, must be based upon the type of cabling. And so on. All three components are necessary for a successful equation.

The most common choices for cable today include coaxial cable, telephone or twisted pair wire, shielded twisted pair and fiber optic. In addition, there are also wireless LANs, which do not use cable at all but rather broadcast their signal from workstation card to server card via radio frequency.

An introduction to terms. Cable pitchmen use a great deal of terminology trying to convince purchasers that their product is the best. Following are three key phrases of the terminology:

- *Attenuation.* How much of the signal is lost over distance. Fiber optic cable has the lowest loss, while, not surprisingly, the greatest loss is with unshielded twisted pair.

- *Bandwidth.* The number of simultaneous transmissions a cable can transport. The greater the bandwidth, the more it can carry, and the lower the bandwidth, the fewer it can carry.

- *Impedance.* The amount of resistance the cable is providing to the transmission it's carrying. Think of impedance as the way gravity reacts to your walking.

Consider the available options. When you're considering adding or expanding a network, you need to consider the whole equation of topology, cards and cable, and include in that equation the physical environment over which you will install the cabling. In older buildings, often you can't get the go-ahead to drill holes in bricks and run fiber optic cable. However, phone lines, which you can use as unshielded twisted pair, may be in place. At the same time, a new building presently under construction offers unlimited possibilities for creating networks.

The cheapest topology for network cabling is Ethernet running across twisted pair wiring. The next cheapest is Ethernet running over coaxial cable. Third comes shielded twisted pair, usually running on token ring. And the most expensive way to network is with fiber optic cable.

Consider using RF if you have to go between two buildings and cannot run a cable. RF, or radio frequency, can be used to link two segments of a network, no matter which topology is involved. If you have a line of sight between the buildings, your choices are to run a laser, microwave or radio link between them. One of the more common choices, due to cost, is NCR's Wavelan, which works quite well from building to building.

When RF is not feasible. If a line of sight is not present, the next best alternative is to lease a "T-1" line from the local telephone company and use a router at each end. These "T-1" lines are dedicated lines that are always active from point A to point B. Their biggest drawback is that they are invariably quite expensive.

Watch for interference. The purpose of shielding cable is to prevent electrical interference to the data being transmitted on the cable. This interference can be caused by almost any electrical device, including motors and ballasts in fluorescent lighting. For this reason, unshielded telephone wire, while the easiest to install, is also the most easily degraded by outside influence.

Avoid interference wherever possible. Never run coaxial or twisted pair cabling near fluorescent lights or electromagnetic devices.

Fiber optic offers several advantages. Fiber optic cabling, while being the most expensive way to go, is also the most secure. With other cables, the transmission is carried in and on the outside of the cable—part of the reason that they are so susceptible to interference from outside sources. With fiber optic cabling, the transmission is carried by light shining through the cable itself, which makes the transmission not nearly as likely to accept degradation.

Additionally, you can use analyzers to see what is being carried on a wire without tapping into the wire if it is not a fiber optic line. This capability is attributable to the carrying of a transmission on the outside of the wire. With fiber optic, someone attempting to tap into the network and ascertain passwords or other guarded information must cut into the line, increasing the likelihood that he or she will not be able to go undetected.

Connectors. Where each cable connects to the server or to a workstation, there must be a connector. Following are the most popular types of connectors:

Type	Description
BNC	Connectors used on Thin Ethernet coaxial cable and ARCnet.
RJ-11	The standard modular telephone connection that supports up to four wires.
RJ-45	Modular telephone style connectors that hold more than four wires—usually eight.
Straight tip	Used on fiber optic cables.
Transceiver	The go-between that transfers data between the backbone network cable and the workstation when it is not feasible to connect the workstation directly; used often with Standard, or thick, Ethernet.

The five main types of twisted pair cabling are differentiated by a type number. These numbers are Type 1, Type 2, Type 3, Type 6 and Type 9. Type 3 is the only one that is not shielded.

Be certain the network cable is properly grounded. If you're running wire between buildings, you are creating an open invitation for lightning.

Always use crimp-on connections. As was mentioned earlier, use crimp-on as opposed to screw-on when using thinnet. The screw-on type tends to come loose over time, and one bad connection affects everyone on the network. Also, try to take as much weight off the cable as possible. Do not connect to the back of the NIC card in the computer and then run the cable under a desk leg and hope no one moves the workstation. Build in slack.

Never use tin connectors and Ts. They may be slightly cheaper, but they don't carry the signal consistently as well as other metals. Although silver connections are only slightly more expensive, you will always be better served using connections made of silver or better-grade metal.

Why terminators are necessary. Ethernet terminators absorb the transmission and prevent the signal from reflecting back along the wire. If you're getting many collision errors, use a voltmeter to check the terminators.

If you're having problems with a network, use a scanner to test cable noise and transmission loss. Check the cable for continuity and the terminator for resistance.

Label cables. A quick way to avoid future headaches is to label all cables. Also label all wallplates, if any, and create a map of connections.

Watch cable length. One of the biggest causes of cable problems when adding new workstations is exceeding allowable cable length. Most frequently, the distant workstations will boot up with no problem but lose the network connection often. Know the limitations imposed on your network by the topology and cabling.

OTHER COMPONENTS & CONCERNS

It would be nice if a network consisted only of a server, some cable and a handful of cards, but alas it does not. In addition to obvious items, such as workstations, which I discuss in Chapter 7, "Workstation Wonders," networks now need other devices. In this section, I talk about backup devices, uninterruptible power supplies and other items worthy of consideration with NetWare 4.0.

Look at the environment. The first thing to consider when you're creating a network is the site itself—the environment into which the server and the network are going to go or now exist.

The site should have dedicated power lines and isolated, grounded outlets. The dedicated lines serve to reduce the likelihood of surges and spikes by making certain that no other devices that could generate these disturbances are using the power lines. When electrical objects do get surges or spikes, they dump this unneeded electrical power into their ground. The reason for isolated grounds going to the networking equipment is, again, to make certain that the server's ground is not carrying an electrical surge that was sent down the line from the box fan in Karen's office.

Power protection is a *must* for the server, and it should be considered likewise for all components as well. It is just as easy for Kristin's workstation to take a spike as it is for the server. With a wire connecting all components of the network together, there is little to prevent the spike from traversing the wire and ending up at the server. Budgets usually prohibit dedicated lines and grounded outlets to all workstations, printers and modems, but at the very least you should equip these components with functioning surge protectors.

Don't overlook protection against static electricity. These days, you can easily have carpeting that is chemically treated to not build static. If you have old carpeting, as in an older site, purchase antistatic spray and keep as much of it as possible on hand. Also, look for carpet pads for chairs to roll on that connect to electrical grounds and dissipate built-up static to the earth.

Read information that comes with your server and check for restrictions on the operating environment in terms of temperature and humidity. Heat dissipation is another item of concern. How much heat does the server generate in the course of continuous operation, and how much air does it need to remain below the operating temperature threshold? You need to consider all of these items to ensure as optimal an operating environment as possible.

Test all cabling and connectors. Do this before putting them into use. It doesn't matter whether this installation is new or whether you're just adding another workstation to the network. You can save many a headache by knowing that the components are in working order before you add them to the network.

Label everything. You should mark clearly all cables as to where they come from and where they go. If it's not feasible to mark each individual cable, make a map and keep it handy.

Cut as few corners as possible. Pay particular attention when it comes to backup peripherals. No matter how enterprising the software is, backups always constitute a pain to the person who has the job of backing up on a regular basis. The more expediently you can back up, the more likely you'll back up on that regular basis.

Consider server-based backups. Server-based backup systems are faster than their counterparts that run from a workstation. The reasons for this discrepancy are fairly obvious. At the server, the data is mirrored and transferred directly to the medium. With workstation devices, the server must send everything to be backed up across the network wire. In addition to being slower, the workstation backup system increases the traffic on the network and slows down all other users who are accessing the server.

Avoid non-standard equipment. When you're considering tape devices, avoid those devices that are not QIC 120-, QIC 80- or QIC 40-compliant. Quarter-Inch Cartridge (or QIC) tape devices, like everything else, are not prone to failure. But, if one fails when you need to perform a restore operation, locating another drive that is compliant with the QIC standard is easier than locating one that is not.

NetWare 4.0 supports only 1/4 inch, 4mm and 8mm tape media for backup. Neither stackers nor magazines are now supported in the NetWare 4.0 backup routine.

Look for SMS-compliant equipment. If you have tape software that is SMS-compliant, you can back up and restore to the tape files that have been compressed after their six days of not being accessed. Other tape devices that are not SMS-compliant require the server to decompress the files in RAM during the backup procedure. Decompressing the files uses up memory and slows down the server considerably.

Plan on workstation backups. Along the backup vein, it is also a good idea to invest in a portable tape device that you can use at workstations to back up the files stored there. Several of the available devices do not require additional cards and can connect directly to the parallel port of the workstation, backing up the contents of the hard drive at an approximate rate of 9mb per minute.

In the old days, users were encouraged to keep copies of their workstation files on the server. That way, when the server was backed up, their workstations were effectively backed up as well. In a small workplace with three or four users, this may still be a viable backup method, but those small workplaces should not be using NetWare 4.0. In a networked environment of 1,000 users, you cannot afford the server storage space that would be lost to users backing up this way, nor can you afford the increase in backup time. It is better to purchase good parallel tape devices and let users perform their own backups.

Anticipate power fluctuations. After you spend huge amounts of money on a file server, cards and cabling, you should never overlook one piece of hardware: the uninterruptible power supply, or UPS. Nothing ruins a NetWare operating system as quickly as power fluctuations.

NetWare 4.0 has a loadable module which can be run from the server that will monitor the status of a UPS and act accordingly. Definable parameters tell it how long the UPS will operate and what time period is necessary to fully recharge it. When the power goes out and the UPS kicks on, NetWare begins the countdown. If the power does not come back on within the given time frame, files are closed and the network is shut down.

If your budget can withstand it, consider buying UPSs for key workstations as well. If the power to a building fails, keeping the server up and running if no workstations can access it serves little purpose. The only real purpose then becomes to shut down the server in an orderly fashion. Bear in mind, however, that file changes that were made by workstations which were suddenly lost run a small risk of being damaged. With many workstations, a solution more feasible than expensive UPS units is a backup generator.

Monitor the temperature. After you spend money on the UPS and grounding equipment, consider an air conditioner. This option ties back in with the operating environment and temperature ranges of the server; some of the new Superservers contain heat sensors that tell you when they are getting too warm. The only solution is to cool them down, and there are two ways of doing so: 1. Reduce the heat with a cooling device, and 2. Turn off the server and let it cool down. Obviously, the latter solution is rarely a legitimate alternative to the former.

Don't forget the CD-ROM player. NetWare 4.0, at this time, does not come with printed manuals. There has been some discussion of printing manuals, but for now all text is included on a CD-ROM disk. You must read or print it with an appropriate player that supports ISO 9600 formatted CD-ROM disks.

CD-ROM networking solutions fall into one of two categories: redirectors and NLM-based. Redirectors require redirector software on the workstation as well as other device drivers and utilities. NLM-based, on the other hand, make networked CD-ROM drives appear as volumes that have been mounted.

All CD-ROM drives are far slower than hard drives, and reading the text directly from the player is a slow process. For this reason, disk caching is included to improve speed and make it practical, as opposed to possible, for multiple users to share access to the drive.

You can view the electronic text manual on a workstation that is equipped with a CD-ROM player, as opposed to through the server, if you have a workstation that meets the necessary requirements. The requirements are a color monitor, a minimum of 4mb RAM (and recommended 6 or 8mb) and a copy of Microsoft Windows 3.x.

You can install the NetWare 4.0 operating system from the CD-ROM. If you elect to do so, you need two SCSI drives for installation, but only one thereafter.

Be sure to buy a CD-ROM that is compatible. A complete list of CD-ROM players endorsed by Novell is on the Electro-text documentation, which you need a CD-ROM player to read, or is available on NETWIRE or by calling Novell at 1-800-NOVELL.

Don't overlook a compatible printer. In addition to the equipment you need to view the electronic text from the CD-ROM, if you wish to print some of the manual, you must add a PostScript printer to your list of required items.

MOVING ON

At the beginning of this book, you saw what was new in NetWare 4.0. In this chapter, you learned the hardware requirements for the network. Now that you know the backbone of the network, it's time to move on to the meat and potatoes and learn about the operating system itself.

Chapter 2, "Menu Magic," will show you how to use the new menus that have been added in Netware 4.0, as well as the handful that have been carried over from previous versions. After the menus are uncloaked, Chapter 3, "Command-line Sorcery," will discuss the command line, and on we go from there.

Chapter 2

MENU MAGIC

One of the strong points of NetWare has always been its menu-style utilities, which allow an administrator to add new users or objects. With NetWare 4.0, Novell has strengthened this benefit even more. With more objects to be managed, Novell had to add more menus, and some of the old ones that existed in versions 2.x and 3.x became obsolete.

The two most important menu utilities are NETADMIN—a new entry used to govern the creation and management of objects—and FILER. FILER, a carryover from the early days of NetWare, governs the attributes and rights of files and subdirectories. Pay particular attention to these two utilities as you read this chapter.

Many of the options that you can perform via the menus you also can complete from the command line, but that information will come in the next chapter. In this chapter, I will discuss the available menus and what you can accomplish through them.

Following are the new menu utilities:

- NETADMIN

- NETUSER

- PARTMGR

- PSETUP

Menu utilities that existed in previous versions and have carried over are as follows:

- COLORPAL

- FILER

- MENU

- PCONSOLE

- PRINTCON

Use the help keys. With most of the menu utilities, you can press F1 for a help screen. Further, pressing F10 usually completes an action, while pressing Esc exits you from one menu to the previous one if you are layered within the menu structure. If you are at the main screen of the menu, pressing Esc will usually exit you out of the utility.

When lists of items or objects are involved, pressing Ins will let you add to the list from wherever the cursor was when you pressed it, and pressing Del will remove the object that the highlight was on.

NEW MENU UTILITIES

A brief discussion of the new menu utilities that were added in this version follows.

NETADMIN

NETADMIN is *the* utility for network administrators. All the functions that you can perform with it pertain to establishing and managing the global network. You use NETADMIN to create *objects*—the term used for any item within the network. You can create users, print queues, subdirectories and everything in between. After you've created these items, you then can use NETADMIN to assign or change the rights and properties associated with them.

Create container objects. You can use NETADMIN to create container objects to hold directory trees. You can create three different types of containers:

- Country objects

- Organization objects

- Organizational Unit objects

To create container objects, choose Manage Objects from the menu (as shown in Figure 2-1) and select the container in which you want to insert another container. Press Ins and choose which of the three types of containers you wish to create. Next, type the object name and press F10 to save the information.

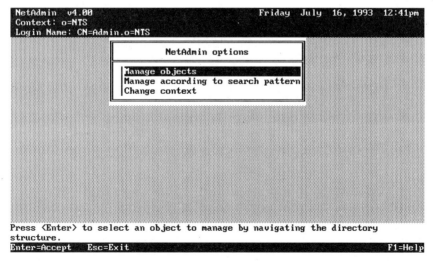

Figure 2-1: The NETADMIN utility lets network administrators use a DOS menu format for managing a NetWare 4.0 network.

Creating new users. Adding new users to the network is a straightforward process that takes very little time. To add new users, choose Manage Objects from the menu; then select the container into which you wish to add the new user. Press Ins and choose User from the menu that appears. Type the new user's first name and then press Enter.

Press F10 and a list of last names for current users on the system appears. Assuming the user you've just added does not have the same last name as someone else, press Ins and type in the new user's last name. If the user will be using more than one last name (maiden, married and so on), continue to press Ins and type in additional names.

When you're finished with the last name entries, press F10 to arrive at the User Identification screen. Make any changes that are necessary and press F10 once more, followed by Esc to return successfully to the main menu. (See Figure 2-2.)

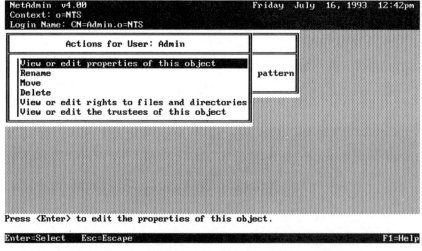

Figure 2-2: NETADMIN lets network administrators manage user functions.

Assigning groups. After you've added users, you should assign them to groups to allow them to have the same permissions to files and directories as other users they interact with.

To add users to a group object, choose Manage Objects from the main menu; then use the arrow keys to find and highlight the group object. Press F10 and the Actions for Group screen appears (see Figure 2-3). Choose View or Edit Object Properties, then choose Group members.

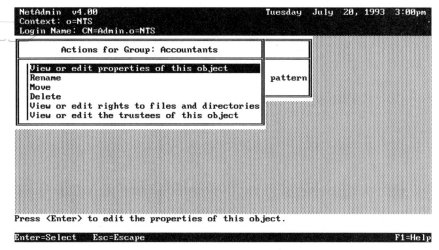

```
NetAdmin  v4.00                        Tuesday  July  20, 1993  3:00pm
Context: o=NTS
Login Name: CN=Admin.o=NTS

       Actions for Group: Accountants

   View or edit properties of this object             
   Rename                                       pattern
   Move
   Delete
   View or edit rights to files and directories
   View or edit the trustees of this object




   Press <Enter> to edit the properties of this object.

 Enter=Select    Esc=Escape                               F1=Help
```

Figure 2-3: The Actions for Group screen lets NetWare 4.0 administrators manage groups on the network.

Press Ins, type in the name of the user to be added to the group and then press Enter. Finally, press Esc to go back to the main menu.

Removing users from groups. If you need to remove a user from a group object—due to termination, transfer or simply no longer needing access to the same files as others—then delete in the following manner.

Choose Manage Objects and then use the arrow keys to find the group object within the highlight. Press F10 and the Actions for Group screen appears. Choose View or Edit Object Properties and then choose Group Members. Highlight the name of the user to remove and press Del. NetWare will ask for a "Y" or "N" response. Press Y and then press Enter to confirm the deletion. Finally, press Esc to go back to the main menu.

Create templates to quicken the process. You can create user templates to give new users a package of benefits when their login is created. Using templates saves you from having to go into every new person's setup and making repetitive changes.

To create user templates, choose Manage Objects from the Options menu. Highlight the object to contain the template and press F10. Choose View or Edit Object Properties and then choose Edit Template User (see Figure 2-4). Type in the values on the screen provided; then press F10 to save, followed by Esc to return to the main menu.

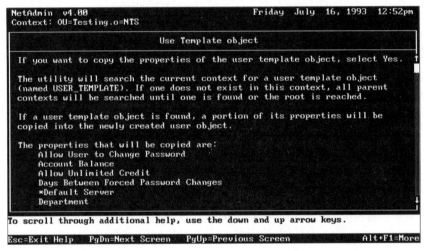

```
NetAdmin  v4.00                            Friday  July  16, 1993  12:52pm
Context: OU=Testing.o=NTS
┌──────────────────────────────────────────────────────────────────────┐
│                          Use Template object                           │
├──────────────────────────────────────────────────────────────────────┤
│  If you want to copy the properties of the user template object, select Yes. │
│                                                                        │
│  The utility will search the current context for a user template object │
│  (named USER_TEMPLATE). If one does not exist in this context, all parent │
│  contexts will be searched until one is found or the root is reached.   │
│                                                                        │
│  If a user template object is found, a portion of its properties will be │
│  copied into the newly created user object.                            │
│                                                                        │
│  The properties that will be copied are:                               │
│      Allow User to Change Password                                     │
│      Account Balance                                                   │
│      Allow Unlimited Credit                                            │
│      Days Between Forced Password Changes                              │
│      *Default Server                                                   │
│      Department                                                        │
└──────────────────────────────────────────────────────────────────────┘
 To scroll through additional help, use the down and up arrow keys.
─────────────────────────────────────────────────────────────────────────
Esc=Exit Help    PgDn=Next Screen    PgUp=Previous Screen        Alt+F1=More
```

Figure 2-4: NETADMIN lets network administrators create multiple users without reentering the same data.

Create aliases. You can create alias objects in a similar manner to other objects, allowing you to reference those objects by other names. An example would be a printer that could be referred to by two names.

To create an alias object, choose Manage According to Search Pattern from the Options menu. Using the Down arrow, highlight Show Alias Class and press Y. Press Enter, then Esc and finally F10 to save the current changes.

Next, choose Manage Objects and look for the name of the container in which you wish to add an alias. After you highlight the name, press Ins and choose Alias. Type the new alias name and press Enter once more.

Next, after the Aliased Object box appears, press Ins and use the arrow keys to move through the directory listing until you find the object you are aliasing. Then press F10 to save and press Esc to return to the main menu. Not nearly as hard as it sounds!

Organizational roles are aliases for a subset of users. Organizational roles are positions users hold as opposed to the individual users themselves. For example, vice president is an organizational role that can be fulfilled by the Vice President of Finance and the Vice President of Operations, as well as of Sales, Marketing and so on. Creating an object for these roles makes them interchangeable in that any one person holding that position fulfills the requirements of the role and can be addressed by position.

To create organizational role objects, choose Manage Objects from the options on the main menu. Highlight the object to contain the organizational role object and press Ins. Choose Organizational Role from the list that appears and type the new organizational role object name. Then press Enter. Type in the values on the screen provided; then press F10 to save the new entry, followed by Esc to return to the main menu.

Profile objects are subsets of users. The subsets are of users for whom a separate login script runs. For example, if members of every department get together on Friday night for bowling, then you can establish a profile object for members of the bowling team not based upon job or department. When these users log in, a special login script can display messages telling them where the next practice is and so on. After the profile login runs, their regular user login runs.

To create profile objects, choose Manage Objects from the Options menu. Highlight the object to contain the profile object; then press Ins and choose Profile. Type a name for the profile and press Enter. Next, type in the values on the screen provided and then press F10. From here you can enter login scripts (which will be addressed in Chapter 4, "File Wizardry"), and when you're finished, press F10 to save, followed by Esc to return to the main menu.

Delete old objects. It is all well and good to create objects, but there will always be those objects that have outlived their usefulness or are no longer needed. When such is the case, it's time to delete objects.

To delete objects from the server, choose Manage Objects from the Options menu. Highlight the object to be deleted and press F10. Choose Delete from the Actions menu that appears; then press Esc to return to the main menu.

Map drives to increase your search path. To create mapping to drives and search drives, choose Manage Objects. Highlight the mapping you want and press F10, followed by Ins. Choose Directory Map from Select an Object Class and type the name for the directory map. Then press Enter.

Add Volume Names to the hard drive. At Volume Name, press Ins and type in the name of the volume object. At the Path field, press Ins and enter the path of the directory. Then press F10.

Modify login scripts. Although login scripts are covered in detail in Chapter 4, knowing how to modify login scripts that already exist is useful. To modify login scripts, choose Manage Objects. Find the desired object and press F10. Choose View or Edit Object Properties and then choose Login Scripts. Enter the commands and press F10.

Copy existing login scripts. To copy a login script from one user or group to another, choose Manage Objects. Then choose View or Edit Object Properties, followed by Login Script. Press F5 to mark the desired text. Next, press Del to remove the script and place a copy of it into memory; then press Ins to restore the text back into place. Finally, press Esc and NetWare will tell you that changes have been made and ask if you would like to save them. In reality, no changes have been made. You have deleted and then restored what was there when you first went into the script. Not saving changes will leave the script the way it was before you entered this section.

Say No to saving changes (press N). Choose Manage Objects, pick a target and then press Ins to insert the script that now exists in memory into this script. Finally, press F10 to save.

Use intruder detection lockout to keep out any user who cannot enter a valid password. To lock out intruders, choose Manage Objects from the main menu. Highlight the container object and press F10. Then choose View or Edit Object Properties from the Actions for screen. Choose Intruder Detection Lockout from the View or Edit screen. Set the options that you want and press Esc to save the settings.

Available options on the Intruder Detection Lockout screen include the following:

- *Detect Intruders.* When set to yes, this option keeps track of the number of incorrect login attempts.

- *Login Intruder Limit.* This option determines the maximum number of wrong tries that a user can make before he or she is then locked out.

- *Interval for Intruder Attempt Reset (D/H/M).* This option determines how long in days, hours and minutes the suspected intruder is to be locked out before NetWare is to reset the flag and let the user log in once more.

- *Lockout After False Detection.* When set to yes, this option locks out any user after he or she exceeds the number of incorrect tries.

- *Interval for Intruder Lockout Reset (D/H/M).* This option determines when the lockout is reset in terms of days, hours and minutes.

Disable lockout to allow a user to log in. When a user can't get logged in because he or she has incorrectly entered his or her password too many times, you must change the lockout status.

To change the status, choose Manage Objects from the main menu. Then highlight the object (usually a user) and press F10.

Choose View or Edit Object Properties from the Actions for User screen. Next, choose Account Restrictions from the View or Edit User screen. Select Intruder Lockout Status from the Account Restrictions screen; then make the desired changes. Finally, press Esc to exit and let the user log in.

Know the Lockout screen. When you look at the Intruder Lockout Status screen, you are viewing a wealth of information, including the following:

- *Account Locked.* If this field is marked, then it is disallowing the user to log in.

- *Incorrect Login Count.* This field counts the number of times the user has unsuccessfully tried to log in to the system.

- *Account Reset Time.* This field determines when lockout status would be automatically reset with no intervention.

- *Time Until Reset.* This field tells you how much of the lock time is remaining.

- *Intruder Address.* If the login is locked, then this field tells you the network and node address the suspected intruder was last using.

Assign account balances to limit server usage. Using NET-ADMIN, you can assign each user an account balance that determines how much service the user can use. But the user must log out and log in again before the changes take place.

NETUSER

NETUSER is version 4.0's replacement for the previous menu utility called Session. With NETUSER, you can set up print jobs, manage drive settings, access network attachments and send messages to other users on the network.

PARTMGR

PARTMGR, as the name implies, is the partition manager utility, which allows the administrator to create partitions. Once partitions exist, you can use the utility to manage and merge partitions of the database.

The main menu of this utility consists of only two choices:

- Manage Partitions

- Change Context

The second choice lets you set your current context, whereas the first offers five additional options:

- Split Partitions

- Merge Partitions

- Add Replicas

- Delete Replicas

- Modify Replicas

The context is your present work environment, while replicas are duplicate portions of the NDS database stored on different servers.

PSETUP

You use PSETUP to set up the printing services. Utilizing it, you can install printing and create the print server object, printer object and the print queue object.

MENU UTILITIES CARRIED OVER FROM PREVIOUS VERSIONS

In addition to the new utilities, many of the older ones that existed in previous versions have been carried over. Some of them were left unchanged from their original functions, while others have had additional capabilities incorporated into them.

COLORPAL

Using COLORPAL, you can change the colors used for other
menu utilities.

FILER

FILER and NETADMIN constitute the two most important menu
utilities to system administrators. Whereas NETADMIN governs
the attributes of objects, FILER creates and manages all aspects of
directories, subdirectories and files, including changing attributes
and trustees.

Following are the FILER options:

1. Manage files and directories.

   Modify, add or view files.

   Change current directory or server.

   Modify, add or view directories.

   Modify, add or view subdirectories.

   Modify, add or view rights for files and directories.

   Modify, add or view trustees for files and directories.

2. Manage according to search pattern.
   This option allows you to view files or subdirectories
   according to search criteria.

3. Select volume object.
   This option allows you to set your current context and
   volume object.

4. View volume information.
   This option shows owner, creation date, creation time,
   volume type, total kilobytes available, maximum directory
   entries and number of entries available.

5. Salvage deleted files.

6. Purge deleted files.

7. Set default filer options.
   This option lets you change confirmation defaults when
   you modify files, file attributes and extended attributes.

Create subdirectories to separate executable files from data and text files. Separating files into subdirectories makes it easier to do incremental backups by only doing so on subdirectories containing information that changes.

To create subdirectories, choose Manage Files and Directories from the Options menu. Choose the volume, directory or subdirectory in which you want to make another subdirectory and then press F10. Type in the name of the new subdirectory and press Enter. Finally, press Esc to return to the main menu.

Add new trustees to existing lists to give users similar rights. To add trustees, choose Manage Files and Directories from the main menu; then find the item you want within the single line highlight and press F10. Choose View/Set File Information and press Enter. Move the arrow key until the highlight is on Trustees and press Enter. Next, press Ins and type the new trustee name. Press Ins twice and find the trustee's name in the list; then press F10.

Eventually the time comes when you must delete a trustee. To do so, choose Manage Files and Directories. Then find the item you want and press F10. Choose View/Set File Information and press Enter. Next, move the arrow keys until the highlight is on Trustees and press Enter. Press Del at the trustee name. Choose Yes and then press Esc to return to the main menu.

As trustees change, change their rights. To modify existing trustee rights, choose Manage Files and Directories. Then find the item you want and press F10. Choose View/Set File Information and press Enter. Next, move the arrow keys until the highlight is on Trustees and press Enter. Press Enter at the desired trustee name and current existing rights appear. Press Ins to add. Press F5 to highlight what you want to add from the list that appears; then press Enter. Finally, press Esc to return to main menu.

Change file attributes to safeguard operations on it. To change the existing attributes of a file or subdirectory, choose Manage Files and Directories. Then find the item you want and press

F10. Choose View/Set File Information and press Enter. Next, move the arrow keys until the highlight is on Attributes and press Enter. Press Del to remove an existing attribute or press Ins to add one. Finally, press Esc to return to the main menu.

Change owners as need be. To change the present owner of an existing directory or file, choose Manage Files and Directories. Then find the item you want and press F10. Choose View/Set File Information and press Enter. Next, move the arrow keys until the highlight is on Owner and press Enter. A list of known users appears. Highlight the user you wish to be the new owner and press Enter. Finally, press Esc to return to main menu.

View trustee rights to verify they are what you think they should be. To view existing trustees' rights for a file or directory, choose Manage Files and Directories. Then find the item you want within the highlight and press F10. Choose View/Set File Information and press Enter. Next, move the arrow keys until the highlight is on Trustees and press Enter. A list of known trustees for the file or subdirectory appears, along with the object type and the current rights each trustee has. Press Esc to return to the main menu.

View and verify information relevant to files is correct. To view current information regarding a file or subdirectory, choose Manage Files and Directories. Then find the item (file or subdirectory) you want and press F10. Choose View/Set File Information and press Enter. Information showing the owner, trustees, attributes, rights, name, file size and date created appears. Press Esc to return to main menu.

Deleted files are not really removed. When files are deleted on a NetWare drive, they are merely marked for deletion and removed from the directory listing functions. In reality, they still exist on the drive and can be recovered if they were erased in error. The only way to remove files completely is to purge them.

You can use FILER to recover deleted (but not purged) files in the following manner. First, choose Salvage Deleted Files from the Options menu. Then choose View and salvage.

Delete those files you truly no longer need. To actually remove files from the server drives, you must purge them. First, choose Purge Deleted Files from the main menu and a prompt for specification occurs. Enter a specification and press Enter. For example, to delete all files that end with the extension TXT, the specification is *.txt.

Be alert when purging. If you do not enter a specification when you're purging files, the default of *.* takes precedence, and all files that have been deleted are permanently removed.

MENU

Menu is a utility that is worthy of discussion here because you can use it to create a simplified, working environment for users by compiling ASCII documents into executable form. Menu systems created with earlier versions of NetWare can convert over to 4.0.

There are some restrictions that govern these utilities; namely, menu programs can go to a maximum of 10 menu levels deep and can contain a maximum of 255 menu screens. The name of each menu can be up to 40 characters long, and the items listed as choices within the menu can be up to 60 characters in length. The main menu must be at the beginning of the source file, and if a command wraps to another line, you must type a + (plus sign) at the end of the line that is to continue. Lastly, menu numbers can be between 1 and 255, and each call within a menu must be to another number.

Following are commands that you can use within the menu programs:

- *MENU*. Marks the beginning of a new menu.
- *ITEM*. Identifies an item to be listed on the menu.

- *EXEC*. Tells DOS to execute an item.

- *LOAD*. Calls a submenu from a different menu program.

- *SHOW*. Displays a submenu from the same menu program.

- *GETO*. Requests optional information from the user before the menu item is executed.

- *GETR*. Requests required information from the user before the menu item is executed.

Following are MENU item options:

- *BATCH*. Removes the menu program from memory before executing an item, freeing an additional 32k.

- *CHDIR*. Changes to the drive and directory in effect before an item is executed.

- *NOCLEAR*. Leaves the present screen display.

- *NOECHO*. Does not echo the commands.

- *PAUSE*. Stops the display and waits for acknowledgment.

- *SHOW*. Displays the commands being executed (the opposite of NOECHO).

Following is an example of a simple menu:

```
MENU 1, Main Menu
  ITEM UNXCLASS
    exec UNXCLASS.EXE
  ITEM DATABASES {NOCLEAR}
    Show 10

MENU 10, DATABASE MENU
  ITEM Q&A
    EXEC QA4
  ITEM PARADOX
    EXEC PARADOX
  ITEM dBASE
    SHOW 20
```

```
MENU 20, dBASE MENU
  ITEM dBASE III
    EXEC DBASE3
  ITEM dBASE IV
    EXEC DBASE4
  ITEM TUTORIAL {BATCH NOECHO}
    EXEC DBTUTOR
```

It is easy to create menus on the fly. To make a menu, use a text editor to create a file. Then name the file and give it an .SRC extension. Type **MENUMAKE {menu_name}** to convert the .SRC file to a .DAT file.

Menus created with earlier versions can be used with 4.0. To convert menus created with previous versions of NetWare to the new format, type **MENUCVNT {main_menu_filename}** and rename the file to an .SRC extension. Next, run MENUMAKE {menu_name}, and once again a .DAT file is created.

Make menu changes easily. To edit an existing menu, use a text editor to work on the .SRC file and make the needed changes there. After you modify it as needed, then recompile the executable by running MENUMAKE {menu_name}.

Change menu key assignments. Each item in a list is automatically assigned an alphabetic selection, but you can change the item from the default to anything else by using ^ (the caret character). For example,

ITEM UNXCLASS	Appears as choice A
ITEM UNXCLASS {^U}	Appears as choice U

Don't overlook the chance to free up memory as the item executes. To do so, add the following to your program:

```
ITEM UNXCLASS {BATCH}
```

 Note the three special cases in regard to the EXEC command:

▪ *EXEC EXIT.* Exits from the menu to a DOS prompt.

▪ *EXEC DOS.* Goes to the DOS shell wherein the user can type exit to return.

▪ *EXEC LOGOUT.* Logs the user out.

 Each item can have up to a maximum of 100 GET commands. You must, however, limit each prompt to one line. You can have up to 10 prompts in each dialog box. To make the prompt appear in its own dialog box, use a ^ at the beginning of the prompt. For example,

```
GETO ^Load Macros? {} 01,,{}
```

 You can use parameters to start the menu utility with special options. The syntax for doing so is as follows:

```
MENU {menu_name} - {option}
```

where valid options are as follows:

-??	Sets the date format. If none is specified, it uses the country information, if existing, in DOS's CONFIG.SYS file.
-A	Turns off all header information in the main menu, including the date and time.

-S#	Reduces the memory requirements.
-V#	Assigns a vector number other than between 96 and 101, which are the defaults.
-Z	Turns off the zoom feature wherein each menu appears small and then enlarges.

PCONSOLE

Using PCONSOLE, you can view the printing operation and make changes as necessary. One of the most straightforward of all menus, PCONSOLE's outline of the choices is as follows:

1. Change Current NetWare Server
   This option allows you to set your current directory path.

2. Print Queue
   Modify, view or add print queues.
   Modify, view or add print jobs.
   Modify, view or add print queue users and operators.

3. Print Server
   Modify, view or add print servers.
   Modify, view or add printers.
   Modify, view or add printer print queue assignments.
   Modify, view or add print server operators.

4. Printer
   Modify, view or add printers.
   Modify, view or add printer print queues and print server assignments.

PRINTCON

Using PRINTCON, you can change configurations that relate to printing via the following options:

1. Change Current NetWare Server.

   This option allows you to set your current directory path.

2. Edit Print Job Configurations.

   Modify, view or add configurations.

3. Select Default Print Job Configuration.

   You can specify what print job configuration will be used when one is not specified in CAPTURE, NPRINT or PCONSOLE.

MOVING ON

In this chapter, you learned about menu utilities and their roles in the lives of system administrators. Now that you're familiar with the menu utilities and the good things they can accomplish for system administrators, it's time to focus on command-line options to enhance your knowledge. Chapter 3, "Command-line Sorcery," will fulfill this goal.

Chapter 3

COMMAND-LINE SORCERY

etWare's menu utilities offer many options, but there are far more that you can execute from a command-line prompt. Additionally, executing a command at the prompt is quicker than beginning a menu program, proceeding through until you layer through a submenu or two, making the selection you want and then exiting back.

In this chapter, we'll discuss the majority of the commands available, in alphabetic order. The only commands not covered in this chapter are those covered elsewhere, such as CAPTURE, which is covered in Chapter 6, "Printer Enchantment," and the FLAG and RIGHTS commands, covered in full detail in Chapter 5, "Directory & File Incantations."

NetWare 4.0 offers four new utilities that did not exist in previous versions, performing specific tasks that were not available heretofore. In order, they are CX, NLIST, NPRINTER and UIMPORT.

Several utilities that were available in previous versions, namely 2.x and 3.x, became obsolete or dated and were dropped from the new version. They are ACONSOLE, ECONFIG, EMSNETX, HELP, IPX, JUMPERS, NETBIOS, NETX, RPRINTER, SET TIME and XMSNETX.

The next category of utilities existed in previous versions and were incorporated into other utilities in this release. These utilities include the following:

- ATOTAL and PAUDIT were wrapped into AUDITCON, which is covered in Chapter 9, "Miscellaneous Alchemy."

- BINDFIX and BINDREST became DSREPAIR, which is discussed in Chapter 4, "File Wizardry."

- ENDCAP became a part of CAPTURE.

- PURGE, SALVAGE and VOLINFO were rolled into a beefed-up FILER menu utility.

- FLAGDIR and SMODE became one with FLAG.

- ATTACH became a part of MAP.

- FCONSOLE was incorporated into the Monitor NLM, which is discussed in Chapter 9.

- CHKDIR and CHKVOL became NDIR.

- DSPACE, MAKEUSER, SECURITY, SYSCON and USERDEF all rolled into NETADMIN, which is discussed in Chapter 2, "Menu Magic."

- SESSION is now the NETUSER menu utility.

- LISTDIR, SLIST and USERLIST went to NLIST.

- ALLOW, GRANT, REMOVE, REVOKE and TLIST were all incorporated into RIGHTS.

- NBACKUP became SBACKUP.

- The two utilities CASTOFF and CASTON ceased living lives apart and were married into SEND.

The last category of utilities did exist in one or more previous versions and are still in the present release in their same form or slightly modified. These utilities are as follows:

CAPTURE	PSC
DCONFIG	RCONSOLE
FLAG	RENDIR
LOGIN	RIGHTS
LOGOUT	SEND
MAP	SETPASS
NCOPY	SETTTS
NDIR	SYSTIME
NPRINT	WHOAMI
NVER	WSUPDATE

NETWARE COMMANDS

Now that the names of the NetWare commands are out of the way, and we know what generation each command is from, let's begin discussing what purpose they serve.

CAPTURE

You use CAPTURE to reroute a print request from the workstation to the network printer. For complete information on this command, see Chapter 6, "Printer Enchantment."

CX

Using CX, you can view your current ConteXt or location in the directory tree. You also can change the current context or view the containers and leaf objects that exist within the directory tree.

The syntax for the command is as follows:

```
CX [new context] [/R] [/T | /CONT | /A ]  [ /C]
```

where valid options are as follows:

/R	Lists all the containers in existence, beginning at the root level.
/T	Trees downward or lists all containers below the current context.
/CONT	Lists all the containers that are within the current context.
/A	All; used with the /T or /CONT parameter, lists all objects at and below the current context.
/C	Continuously scrolls the display and overrides the default display of showing one screen at a time and asking you to press a key to move on to the next screenful of display.

CX can be likened to the CD and DIR commands in DOS. It works like CD when you're changing directories, and it works like DIR when you're looking at a listing of what is in the current context.

Use CX followed by a space and one period (CX .) This moves you back a layer to the directory of which you are now in a subdirectory of. For example, if you're in OPERATIONS.INTERNAL, using this command moves you back to OPERATIONS.

 To move deeper within subdirectories, only specify the additional move. If you use CX SUPPORT.ANDERSON with the above-mentioned directory, you move forward two layers to OPERATIONS.INTERNAL.SUPPORT.ANDERSON

 Use CX ... to move back three layers. From OPERATIONS.INTERNAL.SUPPORT.ANDERSON, this command would move you back to the OPERATIONS directory.

 Use CX /R to move to the root directory. No matter how many subdirectories deep you are, this command always immediately places you in the root directory.

DCONFIG

You use DCONFIG to change the configuration option of the IPX.COM shell file to match the configuration setting of the network board inside the workstation. You can find this utility on the DOS/DOS ODI Workstation Services disk, which came with NetWare 4.0. The syntax for the command is as follows:

```
DCONFIG IPX.COM SHELL:,number
```

where *number* is the configuration option number of the network board—usually found in documentation accompanying the board.

 You also can use WSGEN to generate a new IPX.COM. This is an alternative method used primarily with diskless workstations.

FLAG

You use FLAG to set attributes of files and directories. For more information on this command, see Chapter 5, "Directory & File Incantations."

LOGIN

LOGIN accesses the network, logs into a file server and runs a login script, if one exists. The syntax is as follows:

```
LOGIN [ server / | tree /] [user] [/option]
```

where options are as follows:

/NS	Runs no script even if one exists.
/S	Runs a specified script and must be followed by the name of the script to run.
/SWAP	Runs external commands from within the login script.
/PR	PRofile, wherein you specify objects within the login script that you want to run.
/TR	Specifies that you want to log into a directory tree.
/B	Specifies a bindery login to a non-4.0 server.

When you log in as a 4.0 user, you need to give your password only once. This will grant access to all network resources available. In the old days, you had to specify each server and log into it with the following command:

```
LOGIN SERVER/LOGIN_NAME
```

Now logging in is taken care of by the NetWare Directory Service, which authenticates the user on all servers.

LOGOUT

LOGOUT exits the network and logs out of the servers. Using LOGOUT without any parameters following exits you from all servers. Using LOGOUT [server] exits you from the specified server only.

MAP

MAP serves many purposes. With it, you can view drive mappings, create network or search drive mappings, change network or search drive mappings and map a fake root drive. The syntax is as follows:

```
MAP [ P | NP ] [option] drive:= [drive:|path]
```

where options are as follows:

P	Physical volume; you must list this parameter on the command line in the first or second position.
NP	No Prompt; overwrites local or search drives without prompting you for action.
DEL	Deletes existing drive mappings.
INS	Inserts a search drive mapping without replacing an existing one.
N	Maps the next available drive.
ROOT	Maps a fake root.

All drive mappings are lost when you log out. If you want to save them, the easiest thing to do is to add them to your login script. Alternatively, you can place them in a batch file that you execute when you need those settings.

 You can have a minimum of no mappings and a maximum of 26 mappings. This maximum includes your local drives.

 Search drive maps always begin with the letter *Z* and work their way backward. You can have up to 16 search drives.

 Enter MAP without parameters. If you use MAP without any parameters, you see the mappings currently in effect for you.

 Use MAP DEL K: to remove the mapping for drive K. This removes only that mapping and leaves all other existing mappings as they were.

 Use MAP K:=SYS:\QA4\KAREND to map drive K to the given directory. This can be done even if a value already exists for K:—rather than needing to delete and reassign a map, you can simply assign a new value.

 Use MAP ROOT G:=HOME\KRISTIN to map drive G as a fake root. Many applications try to write to a root directory, and this command will give them a place from which to operate for this user without truly affecting the root drive of the system.

NCOPY

The NCOPY command copies files from one location to another on this or another network. The syntax is as follows:

```
NCOPY [path] filename [TO] target path [filename] [/option]
```

where allowable options are as follows:

/A	Copies only those files on which the archive or backup bit is set.
/C	Copies the files without preserving the extended attributes and name space information.
/F	Tells the operating system to write sparse files.
/I	Informs you when extended attributes or name space information cannot be copied because the target is not supporting these options (non-4.0).
/M	Copies only archive bit files and turns off that archive bit at the source.
/S	Includes all subdirectories in the copy.
/S /E	Copies empty subdirectories by creating their names on the target.
/V	Verifies that new and old files are identical after the copy is completed.

Wildcard characters are not supported with the NCOPY command.
You cannot use asterisks to stand for any number of characters or question marks to stand for one character. Rather, filenames must be specifically spelled out.

You can use periods to stand for this subdirectory or one further back in the tree. For example, using NCOPY KAREN ../S copies empty subdirectories from two layers back.

NDIR

You use NDIR to obtain a listing of files and directories on the server. For a detailed explanation of this command, see Chapter 5, "Directory & File Incantations."

NLIST

You use NLIST to view information about files, directories, users, groups, volumes, servers, queues, objects and their properties. The syntax is as follows:

```
NLIST [object] [=object name] [/option]
```

where *object* can be a user, server, queue, group or volume; and *object name* is what you want to view information about.

Available options are as follows:

/A	Displays users currently logged in.
/Bindery	Displays information stored in the bindery of pre-4.0 servers.
/C	Continuously scrolls the display.
/CO[=context]	Sets the context to be searched.
/D	Shows all object details.
/N	Displays object names.
/S	Searches all levels.
/SHOW [property]	Displays specific groups of properties.

You also can use the following operators:

EQ	Equal to
LT	Less than
GT	Greater than
NE	Not equal to
LE	Less than or equal to
GE	Greater than or equal to

 To see a list of all users who have passwords of three characters or less in length, use the following command:

```
NLIST USER WHERE "PASSWORD LENGTH" LE 3
```

 To see who is logged in right now, use the following command:

```
NLIST USER /A
```

 To see all properties for Kristin, use the following command:

```
NLIST USER=KRISTIN /D
```

 To see a listing of all groups that have 12 members or more, use the following command:

```
NLIST GROUP WHERE MEMBERS GE 12
```

NPRINT

The NPRINT utility prints an ASCII file or one already formatted for a printer. See Chapter 6, "Printer Enchantment," for more information on this command.

NVER

NVER displays information on the network and attached servers.

PSC

PSC controls the print server and network printers. See Chapter 6 for more information.

RENDIR

Use this self-explanatory utility to rename a directory. The proper syntax for RENDIR is as follows:

```
RENDIR path [TO] directory name
```

 You can use one period to represent the default directory. To illustrate:

```
RENDIR . TO KAREND
```

 You use :/, which represents the current drive and volume. As in the following:

```
RENDIR :/KAREND TO KRISTIN
```

RENDIR does not automatically change any drive mappings that include this path. If you have a drive mapped to a directory that you rename, be sure to change the mapping to the new location name.

RIGHTS

You use RIGHTS to set and view the attributes assigned to files and directories. For more information on this command, see Chapter 5.

SEND

SEND does just what its name implies. It lets you send messages to other users, and it sets the workstation to receive all, only system or no messages at all. It also polls for messages and views them in broadcast mode. The syntax is as follows:

```
SEND {message} {users} [options]
```
where options can be as follows:

/A or /A=A	Accepts all messages (which is the default).
/A=C	Accepts messages only from the server.
/A=N	Accepts no messages, whether they are from other users or the server.
/A=P	Polls for messages.
/P	Polls for stored messages.
/S	Sets broadcast mode.

To send a message to one user, use the following command:

```
SEND "Get Busy" KAREN
```

To send messages to more than one user, separate the names with a comma, as follows:

```
SEND "Time for Lunch" KAREN,KRISTIN
```

Messages can be sent to users on non-4.0 servers. To send the message to a server that is not running NetWare 4.0, you must specify the server, the name of the person the message is going to and "/B" for bindery-based, as follows:

```
SEND "Get a life" BI_ANDERSON/KAREN/B
```

Messages have to be 55 characters in length or less. Any messages over 55 characters are truncated.

 Be careful when sending messages. When you send a message to a user, processing ceases on his or her machine as the message is displayed on the last line of the screen. The user must press Ctrl-Enter to clear the message and restart processing.

If a user starts up a program that requires many calculations and then walks away from the machine only to come back an hour later and find that no processing was done because someone sent a message, he or she may have a tendency to become irate. Hence, you can use the /A=C option, which keeps other users from sending messages but still lets the server report if something needs to be sent.

 You can SEND from the new user tool utility NWUSER or NETUSER in 4.0, as well. See further discussion of these utilities in Chapter 2, "Menu Magic."

SETPASS

Use the SETPASS utility to change your password. Simply type in the command, and then you'll be prompted for the new password. After you type the password, you're asked to retype it to verify that you entered it correctly. If both entries match, the new value becomes the password. If they do not match, the password remains what it was.

 Passwords can be up to 127 characters long but cannot contain control characters. It is a good idea to keep passwords somewhat shorter, usually between 8 and 12 characters.

SETTTS

SETTTS works with your application in tracking a transaction by setting the logical record locks and the physical record locks. This command ensures that the Transaction Tracking System works with the applications to keep track of activity.

SYSTIME

The SYSTIME utility synchronizes the workstation date and time with the server.

Synchronization can be done from other servers. If you don't wish to synchronize with the current server that you are attached to, issue the command followed by the name of the server you want to take the time from. For example, use SYSTIME BOULDER to synchronize with the BOULDER server.

UIMPORT

With the UIMPORT utility, a network supervisor can create many user objects using an optional database, such as Q&A or dBASE, and directly load them into the Directory Services tree from an ASCII import file. The syntax is as follows:

```
UIMPORT [controlfile] [datafile]
```

where *controlfile* is what gives UIMPORT the information on how to load the data into the directory and *datafile* is a comma-separated ASCII file, wherein all fields are enclosed within quotation marks.

Be certain to use proper syntax. If there is a line break between fields within the datafile, the first line must end in a comma (,).

Watch trailing characters. In keeping with the preceding trap, the last field of a record cannot end with a comma.

Avoid quotes. Fields themselves cannot contain quotation marks because they denote the end of one field and the beginning of the next.

You can leave fields blank. If you don't know the value or don't want to use the field, you must account for the space as follows:

, ,

Number fields cannot contain commas. Since commas denote the end of one field and the beginning of the next, the number "1,000" would be interpreted as two fields, "1" and "000".

WHOAMI

WHOAMI gives you connection information, and you can use it with no parameters or with the following parameters:

/B	Shows additional server information.
/C	Continuously displays the information without prompting you to press a key to see the next screen.

WSUPDATE

Use the WSUPDATE utility to update a file on multiple drives and subdirectories. The syntax is as follows:

```
WSUPDATE [source path] [drive letter: | volume name:]
[path\filename] [/options]
```

where options are as follows:

/ALL	Searches all mapped drives.
/C	Copies new files over old ones without backing up the old ones.
/E	Erases the existing log file.
/F=[path\file]	Signifies a file where commands are stored.

/LOCAL	Searches all local drives.
/L=[path\file]	Gives the location and name of a WSUPDATE log file.
/P	Prompts you to proceed.
/O	Updates all files, even those marked read-only.
/R	Renames the old file(s) with .OLD extension.
/S	Updates subdirectories as well.

 To search the mapped drive and copy over the old files, use the following command:

```
WSUPDATE VOL:SYSTEM\EAD.EXE /C
```

MOVING ON

You have now been exposed to menu utilities and command-line options. With this task accomplished, it's time to get a bit more selective and begin looking at topics in terms of what they offer specifically as opposed to generally.

The following chapter, "File Wizardry," will cover administrative functions such as setting up login scripts, performing backups and maintaining security. Read it for an understanding of the environment in which NetWare is operating with each user, server and site.

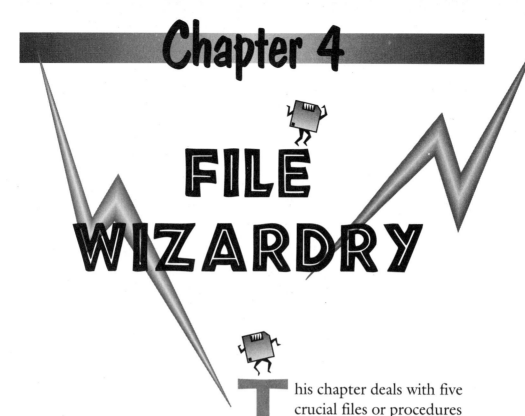

Chapter 4

FILE WIZARDRY

This chapter deals with five crucial files or procedures that relate to the network operation. All the commands and topics are pertinent only to system administrators, because without proper permissions, none of the procedures discussed here pertains to the average user.

We will begin by discussing my favorite topic, login scripts. From there, we'll move to accounting, backups, NetWare Directory Services and end with security—another favorite.

If you're not a system administrator or are not responsible for these five areas, then jump to Chapter 5, "Directory & File Incantations," for a discussion of file and directory attributes and permissions.

LOGIN SCRIPTS

You can use login scripts to set up a user's workstation environment automatically each time he or she logs into the server. Think of login scripts as network counterparts to AUTOEXEC.BAT files in MS-DOS.

Login scripts can perform basically four functions:

- Map drives and search drives to subdirectories.

- Display messages.

- Set environmental variables.

- Execute external programs or menus.

 Three types of login scripts are now supported:

- *System login scripts* set general environments for all the users in an organization or organizational unit.

- *Profile login scripts* set environments for a group of users and execute after the system login script.

- The old stand-by, *user login scripts*, set environments specific to a single user and execute after the other two.

All three types are optional, and you can have one or all of them.

 A login script has no set length. It can be one line or hundreds of lines.

 Scripts are *not* case sensitive. "map" works the same as "MAP" or "Map."

 The maximum line length in a script is 150 characters. It is recommended, however, to stick to 78 or fewer characters so that the whole line will show on the screen.

 You can include only one command on each line. If more than one command is on a line, only the first one is executed.

 Enter lines in the order that you want them to execute. Blank lines have no effect on operation at all, and you can use them to differentiate one section of processing from another—making the script easier to read.

 In the absence of any of the three types of login scripts, the NetWare default login script runs:

```
WRITE "Good %GREETING_TIME, %LOGIN_NAME."
MAP DISPLAY OFF
MAP ERRORS OFF
MAP *1:=SYS:; *1:=SYS:%LOGIN_NAME
IF "%1"="ADMIN" THEN MAP *1:=SYS:SYSTEM
MAP INS S1:=SYS:PUBLIC; INS
    S2:=SYS:PUBLIC\%MACHINE/%OS/%OS_VERSION
MAP DISPLAY ON
MAP
```

 Watch for command replication. Because two or more of the three scripts can execute the same commands, the last one to execute is the one that takes precedence.

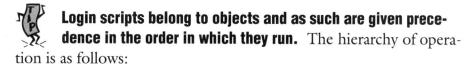 **Login scripts belong to objects and as such are given precedence in the order in which they run.** The hierarchy of operation is as follows:

1. organization = system script

2. organizational unit = system script

3. profile = profile script

4. user = user script

If you upgrade from another version of NetWare to version 4.0, the login scripts from the previous version will carry over. Those that existed for user KAREN will still exist for user KAREN, though there are a few commands that may not be supported any longer—more on those follows.

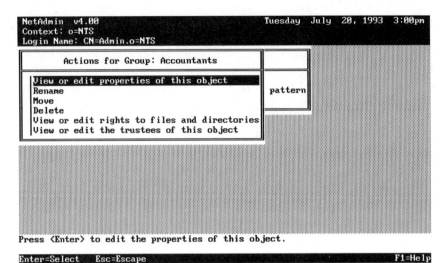

Figure 4-1: A NetWare 4.0 administrator can manage login scripts through NETADMIN or NWADMIN, as shown here. SYSCON does not exist as a separate utility in 4.0.

 Use ATTACH to connect to bindery-based (non-4.0) servers while the login script is running. This enables a user to seamlessly connect to an old server.

Be concious of the BREAK ON command. BREAK ON lets a user press Ctrl-C to break out of the login routine and return to a prompt. Using this command is good when you first create a script and fear that the logic embedded in it may throw it into a loop.

As a rule, however, you do not want a user to be able to break from the script, so use BREAK OFF to disable the Ctrl-C key combination.

DOS BREAK checks the Ctrl-Break checking level for DOS. Specify on or off after the command to toggle the operation. For example, DOS BREAK ON turns on the checking level.

Use CLS in a command to clear the screen. This rids the user of a cluttered display—the same as in DOS.

Make certain the COMSPEC variable is set correctly.
COMSPEC specifies the directory where DOS and the command processor (COMMAND.COM) are loaded if users run their DOS from the network, as with diskless workstations.

Change directories within the login script. CX works the same inside a login script as it does from the command line, and you can use this command to set a user's current context in the directory file.

Use DISPLAY to show the contents of a text file if the file is in ASCII format and non–word processed. If the text file has been word processed, then DISPLAY will show the processing codes. To avoid seeing these codes, use the FDISPLAY command instead.

If you need to set local PC variables from within the script, use DOS SET. This command works in the same manner as the SET command in MS-DOS.

If you need to set several variables, be sure you have enough room in the environment. You can create more environment space on the workstation by calling from inside the workstation's AUTOEXEC.BAT, as follows:

```
COMMAND /E:nnn /P
```

where *nnn* stands for the number of bytes of environmental space you wish to create.

To verify that copy operations can be read on the target without error, use DOS VERIFY ON. To save the extra step, use DOS VERIFY OFF. This procedure works only with the COPY command supplied with DOS and does not work with NetWare's NCOPY command.

Consider default drives. You can specify a default drive for the user by including a DRIVE statement in the login script.

Continue processing after the login script. If you need to
execute a command upon completion of the login procedure,
end the script with an EXIT statement, followed by the name of the
program to run. Program names cannot be more than 14 characters
long and must be executable files or internal DOS commands.

You can use the PCCOMPATIBLE command to enable EXIT to
run if the workstation's machine name is not IBM_PC. This approach
does not apply to OS/2 versions.

**To grab a user's attention when you want him or her to read a
screen display, use the following:**

```
FIRE PHASERS n TIMES
```

where *n* is the number of times for the phaser sound to repeat.

Login scripts need not be processed line by line. Processing
can jump around in a script if you use GOTO and can even be
conditional if you use IF...THEN statements. You can check for the
equality or nonequality of values, using the following operands:

=	Values are equal, as in `IF DAY_OF_WEEK="MONDAY"`.
<>	Values are not equal, as in `IF DAY_OF_WEEK<>"MONDAY"`.
>	The value is greater than.
>=	The value is greater than or equal to.
<	The value is less than.
<=	The value is less than or equal to.

By no means are you limited to commands in the login script.
Use INCLUDE to run commands that are somewhere other than in the login script.

 Create a record of usage. LASTLOGINTIME displays the time of the user's last login.

 Use MACHINE to set the DOS machine name of the workstation.
This command does not, however, work with OS/2.

 You can use MAP in five different ways:

- *MAP DISPLAY on/off.* Tells whether or not the MAP display is shown on the workstation screen. The default is on.

- *MAP ERRORS on/off.* Tells whether the errors are displayed on the workstation screen. The default is on.

- *MAP DEL.* Deletes a mapping, making it available again.

- *MAP INS.* Inserts a drive mapping between two existing ones.

- *MAP ROOT.* Maps a fake root. See Chapter 3, "Command-line Sorcery," for more information.

 Local drives are always A through E. You must begin mapping network drives with F.

 Use the NO_DEFAULT parameter if you do not want the user to use the default user script. Place this command in a system or profile login.

 Stop display scrolling long enough for acknowledgment. If you want processing to wait in a login script so that the user can read the screen, use the PAUSE command.

To make a login script more readable, use REMARK statements. These are skipped by processing when the script is executed. For example, you can add the following:

```
REMARK This Is Where Day Of Week is Checked
```

Keep workstation times the same or different. By default, when a user logs in at his or her workstation, the time on the workstation is set to that of the server. If you do not want this action to take place, use SET TIME OFF.

You can use the SHIFT command to force the processing routine to read the next variable in a list. For example, SHIFT 1 moves the %2 variable into %1, and SHIFT 2 moves the %4 variable into %2. The number following SHIFT can be between 1 and 10.

WRITE is the NetWare equivalent of ECHO. You can use it to send messages to the console, and it can display variables that are preceded by a % and typed in capital letters. For example, you can use the following to display how many days until the user's password expires:

```
WRITE Your password expires in %PASSWORD_EXPIRES days
```

Allowable variables are as follows:

DAY	Shows the day of the month from 1 through 31.
DAY_OF_WEEK	Spells out Monday, Tuesday, etc.
MONTH	Displays the numerical equivalent from 01 through 12.
MONTH_NAME	Displays January, February, etc.
NDAY_OF_WEEK	Shows 1 for Sunday, 2 for Monday, etc.

SHORT_YEAR	Displays 93, 94, 95, etc.
YEAR	Gives four digits; for example, 1993.
AM_PM	Returns which time of day is appropriate.
GREETING_TIME	Offers one of three choices: morning, afternoon or evening.
HOUR	Displays 1 through 12.
HOUR24	Displays 00 through 23.
MINUTE	Displays 00 through 59.
SECOND	Displays 00 through 59.
FULL_NAME	Gives the user's full name.
LOGIN_NAME	Returns the user's login name.
PASSWORD_EXPIRES	Tells how many days before expiration.
USER_ID	Gives the user's ID.
FILE_SERVER	Returns the name of the file server.
NETWORK_ADDRESS	Gives an 8-digit hexadecimal number.
DOS_REQUESTER	Tells the version of the DOS shell.

MACHINE	Displays IBM_PC, etc.
NETWARE_REQUESTER	Tells the version of NetWare.
OS	Tells the operating system type—DOS, etc.
OS_VERSION	Displays 3.3, etc.
P_STATION	Gives the node address in 12-digit hexadecimal format.
SHELL_TYPE	Gives the shell type calling the login script.
SMACHINE	Gives the short machine name.
STATION	Displays the workstation connection number.
ACCESS_SERVER	Returns true if server is functional.
ERROR_LEVEL	Displays any existing error levels after the last function.

 Add further enhancements to displays. You can use \n to write to a new line or \7 to cause the workstation to beep.

To run external programs in .EXE or .COM format, use the pound sign (#) and the program name. The login script stays resident in memory while the # command is executed, then returns and continues where it left off.

You must use COMMAND /C to run an internal DOS command in a login script. Using this option allows you to use the DOS COMMAND.COM to execute one command and then return to the script. Without this option, NetWare looks for a file with an .EXE or .COM extension and nothing more. Use the following:

```
#COMMAND /C DEL C:\KAREN.LST
```

Some login script commands that existed in other versions of NetWare do not exist in 4.0. If you upgrade a server and it contains one of the following commands, you must modify the script:

- *ATTACH.* This command is not supported for 4.0 servers.

- *MEMBER_OF_GROUP.* Groups have been replaced by group objects, so this variable no longer works.

- *MAP.* Mapping to a drive on the Directory Services volume does not require you to include the server name in the MAP command. However, when you map a drive to a server that is running an earlier version of NetWare, you must leave the MAP command the way it was.

ACCOUNTING

NetWare 4.0 took the capabilities of two earlier commands—ATOTAL and PAUDIT—and rolled them into a comprehensive auditing program that allows you to keep track of network resources. This auditing program option is installed automatically during the installation of version 4.0.

 To enable the auditing of a volume, follow these steps:

1. Type **AUDITCON** at any DOS workstation.

2. Choose Enable Volume Auditing from the Available Audit Options menu.

3. Enter a password for the volume.

4. Enter the password again at the prompt.

To enable auditing of Directory Services, follow these steps:

1. Type **AUDITCON** at any DOS workstation.

2. Choose Audit Directory Services from the Available Audit Options menu.

3. Select Audit Directory Tree from the menu by highlighting the container name and pressing F10.

4. Enter a password for the container.

5. Enter the password again at the prompt.

Auditing can be accessed at any workstation. Access any of the options by simply typing **AUDITCON** at a workstation and making your selection from the menu that comes up. You also can change the password, create audit reports and so on.

BACKUPS

In NetWare 4.0, the backup routine has been renamed SBACKUP, and you can use it to take a snapshot of selected data, sort and store the data on a tape, and retrieve it later.

Stackers and magazines are not supported in version 4.0. NetWare now supports *only* tape media for backup operations. Supported sizes are 1/4 inch, 4mm and 8mm. If you're using 4mm tape, use only Digital Data Storage—NDS-certified computer-grade tapes.

Keep spare tapes handy. Because the backup can now span more than one tape, always have extra tapes on hand.

If volume compression is turned on, the restore speed may be degraded if you restore by overwriting existing files. To hasten recovery speed, delete the files that you no longer want on the hard disk before you begin the restore. This way the files are copied in fresh and overwriting is not necessary.

SBACKUP command-line options are as follows:

- Buffer size (size=xxx): the default is 64k but sizes can be 16k to 256k.

- Number of buffers (BUFFER=x): the default is 4 but can be 2 to 10.

SBACKUP can do four types of backups:

- Full

- Differential—all modified since the last backup

- Incremental—all modified since the last full or incremental backup

- Custom—whatever you want

Never combine differential and incremental backups. These serve similar purposes, and you're not getting enough information to restore should the need arise.

Unattended backups always run at the same time. The default time for a delayed backup is midnight of the current day.

Backup the tree. SBACKUP and any backup solution supporting SMS on 4.0 can back up the Directory Services tree because a replica of it resides on every server. During the operation, the tree is logically queried and backed up. Because of this operation, you can back up one server and have the information to restore to any server. You no longer have to back up every server to keep the database intact.

If you have only one server, however, then it becomes crucial that you back it up on a regular basis.

NETWARE DIRECTORY SERVICES DATABASE

The NetWare Directory Services database replaces the bindery and contains information on users and all resources of the network. It does not reside on a single server but instead is replicated on every server across the network, and each server's replica is updated on a routine basis.

 You can use four utilities that can help maintain the NDS database:

- *PARTMGR.* You use the partition manager to make copies, or replicas, of partitions.
- *UIMPORT.* You use this utility to import user objects and properties from existing ASCII databases.
- *DSREPAIR.* You use this utility to check and make repairs to the database.
- *MERGE TREE.* This loadable module creates a single NDS from two separate copies.

Use replicas wherever possible. You make copies of a partition—known as *replicas*—and place them on different servers to make servers more accessible across the network. You also reduce traffic by not having to verify users across the network when you can do it at the local server.

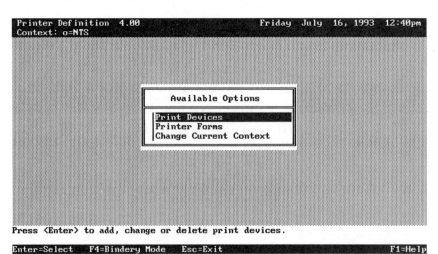

Figure 4-2: NetWare 4.0 administrators should copy partitions onto different network servers.

Bear in mind that replicas also provide fault tolerance. If a server crashes, you can restore a replica from another, and in almost all instances, this approach is much quicker than rooting through backup tapes and restoring from them.

Partitions contain Directory Services database information only. They do not hold any information on files or directories. You must still perform backups to provide fault tolerance for them.

There are three types of replicas: master, read/write and read-only. You can create them only at the container level. You cannot store more than one replica of the same partition on a server.

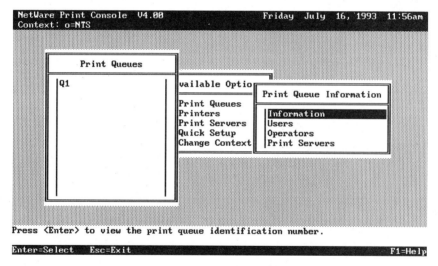

```
NetWare Print Console  V4.00                  Friday  July  16, 1993  11:56am
Context: o=NTS

            Print Queues
        ┌──────────────────────┐  ┌vailable Optio┌────────────────────────────┐
        │Q1                    │  │              │ Print Queue Information     │
        │                      │  │Print Queues  │                             │
        │                      │  │Printers      │┌───────────────────────────┐│
        │                      │  │Print Servers ││Information                 ││
        │                      │  │Quick Setup   ││Users                      ││
        │                      │  │Change Context││Operators                  ││
        │                      │  │              ││Print Servers              ││
        │                      │  └──────────────┘└───────────────────────────┘│
        │                      │
        └──────────────────────┘

 Press <Enter> to view the print queue identification number.

 Enter=Select    Esc=Exit                                             F1=Help
```

Figure 4-3: The partition manager utility PARTMGR lets the network administrator create, manage and duplicate partitions.

To create a new partition, follow these steps:

1. Type **PARTMGR** at the command-line prompt.

2. Choose Manage Partitions (see Figure 4-3).

3. Highlight the container object to partition and press Enter.

4. Answer Yes to the "create new partition?" message by pressing Y.

To merge partitions, follow these steps:

1. Type **PARTMGR** at a command-line prompt.

2. Choose Manage Partitions.

3. Highlight the partition to merge and press Enter.

4. Highlight Merge With Parent Partition and press Enter.

5. Answer Yes to the "create new partition?" message by pressing Y.

To create a replica, follow these steps:

1. Type **PARTMGR** at a command-line prompt.

2. Choose Manage Partitions.

3. Highlight the partition to replicate and press Enter.

4. Highlight View/Edit Replicas and press Enter.

5. Press Ins to add a replica.

6. Enter the information about type and answer Yes to the "create replica partition?" message by pressing Y.

NDS databases can be repaired. To repair the database if it becomes corrupted, run DSREPAIR by going to the corrupted server and typing **LOAD DSREPAIR**.

DSREPAIR works only on the server it is running on. If the corruption is a global problem, you must run the repair utility on all servers individually.

Running DSREPAIR locks the Directory Services database and does not let users access the server. You must exit completely from the program to unlock it and give users access again.

You can use UIMPORT to update user information when records are changed. Chapter 3 provides information on the UIMPORT utility.

SECURITY

Security on a network is a combination of common sense, preventive measures and troubleshooting. Preventive measures deal with known eventualities, while troubleshooting is confronting the unknown. Usually, employing preventive measures and common sense is easier than troubleshooting.

The following tips and traps are common-sense solutions aimed at keeping the network running as long as possible by reducing the risks of corruption by users or outsiders purposely acting inappropriately.

Lock the server where it cannot be seen or touched by anyone but the system administrator. A server sitting in the open is an invitation for anyone to approach it. The server keeps the network running, and if an overzealous user begins testing commands he or she heard about from Aunt Lorraine's son Tony, who is a CNE in Grand Rapids, then trouble is sure to follow.

Run SECURE CONSOLE. When activated on the server, it keeps NLMs from loading anywhere but under servername/SYS:. This procedure prevents keyboard entry into the debugger and prevents anyone other than the console operator from changing the date and time on the server.

Be aware of viruses. Viruses are to the computer world what caffeine was to soft drinks several years ago. At the mere mention of their name, grown men begin to quiver and shake. They wring their hands behind their backs so that you won't see their fingers crossed in hopes that their systems escape "just one more time," and they sulk away with heads hung low.

Although no system is virus-immune, you can shorten the effects on an infected system by doing frequent backups. Rotate backups and keep many days past before overwriting the tapes. This way, if you find an infection on Friday and you know that it was there on Wednesday, you can go back and still find Monday's tapes to load.

Keep a write-protected, bootable disk handy just in case your situation degrades to that point. And utilize virus-scanning routines, which you can obtain for very reasonable prices. Finally, keep backups of executable files, and flag them with the X attribute.

If your hardware supports it, use a power-up password on the server. When the user boots up, he or she must supply a password before the operating system is loaded.

Good fences make good neighbors, and good passwords can keep prying eyes out of a system. You've seen reams of paper telling you not to use first names, last names or the name you go by when you frequent underground pubs on the seedy side of town.

In brief, never use passwords less than six characters in length or ones that are easily guessed. Change your password often, and never write it down. Mix and match numbers and letters, and the more permissions you have, the more important it is to follow the rules.

For an intruder to log in, he or she must know two things: the name of a user object and a password. If you are a system administrator, you can increase the security of each user's login by setting several options:

- By default, passwords are not required on a system. Change this option to Yes by toggling an X in the check box.

- Set the minimum password length to 6. Whereas the maximum is 127 for DOS-based machines, it is only 10 on Macintosh workstations. So if you set password length too high, you will make establishing passwords difficult for Mac users.

- Set Periodic Change in Passwords to Yes. The default time is 90 days, which should be sufficient for most sites.

- Turn on the Unique Password option. Setting this option causes NetWare to remember the last eight passwords that were used for at least one day for each user and forces the users to create a different one when changing passwords.

 Don't overlook the possibilities of using passwords within applications. Many programs offer password protection on the files they generate, which provides an extra layer of protection for that data.

Some applications write files to the root drive. This capability goes against every grain of security etiquette. Use MAP ROOT to assign a fake root to which the user can be assigned rights.

When you're considering security, don't overlook the following:

- *ATTRIBUTES.* For files and directories.

- *EFFECTIVE RIGHTS.* A combination of the object's trustee assignments and inherited rights.

- *INHERITANCE.* The rights granted to a trustee by a trustee assignment apply to everything below that point. You can block this attribute with an Inherited Rights Filter attribute.

- *RIGHTS.* For files and directories.

- *TRUSTEES.* PUBLIC is a special trustee; if a user tries to access a directory or file without any other rights, he or she will be assigned whatever PUBLIC dictates.

Use filters with care. Be careful not to block everyone's rights with an Inherited Rights Filter, leaving no one with access to the directory tree.

Security equivalence is a powerful tool to use with all due caution. If a user has rights to add to his or her own security equivalence list, he or she is able to add the name of the network administrator and change everything on the network.

Remember timed synchronization. One large security concern is if a user quits and you disable his or her account on a WAN with many servers. That user can still log in at a distant server until the replica on that server is synchronized with the current server.

The synchronizing of Directory Service replicas is not a configurable option but rather an ongoing process. When you make a change to any server, that server is responsible for updating all the other replicas of the partition, meaning all the other servers. The former user may still be able to log in remotely if the remote server has not been updated, but he or she will be unable to access information stored on any server that has been updated.

MOVING ON

This chapter covered five administrative topics and discussed how they apply to the network. In Chapter 5, "Directory & File Incantations," you will learn how to list files in a directory as well as set the attributes and rights for the files and directories.

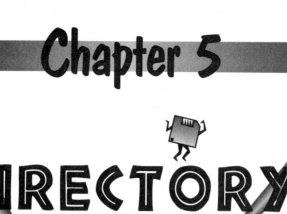

Chapter 5

DIRECTORY & FILE INCANTATIONS

hen networks were first created, they served two purposes. The first was to share peripherals; hence, you could have one nice printer connected to a server, and everyone on the network could use that printer. This setup saved the cost of buying a nice printer for every workstation, not to mention the space savings.

The second purpose was to enable all users on the network to share information in the form of files and directories. If everyone had access to the same information, then databases could be kept up to date and users could work more effectively with the shared data.

What started out as a few shared databases has grown or, more appropriately, evolved into a very crucial component of the network. How the files and directories are set up and maintained has every bearing on security, functionality and operation. In this chapter, we will talk about the outline of a directory tree, object and property rights, attributes, FLAG, RIGHTS and NDIR.

PLANNING & PLANTING A DIRECTORY TREE

The directory tree is the governing body by which a NetWare 4.0 network operates. Naturally, the more efficiently you plan the directory tree, the easier it will be for the network to operate, be maintained and grow. The importance of proper initial planning and design cannot be stressed enough.

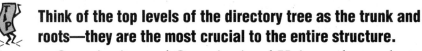 **Plan the directory tree to get the most conservative use out of all your network resources.** If you have fewer than five servers, I would advise you to have only one directory tree. If you have more than five servers, then I recommend you create two or more trees to take the utmost advantage of the NetWare Directory Services.

Think of the top levels of the directory tree as the trunk and roots—they are the most crucial to the entire structure. Country, Organization and Organizational Unit are the top layers.

Plan for expansion. Because you cannot insert a level into a tree after it is created, I highly recommend that you create more levels than you need now and allow room for expansion.

Conversely to the preceding tip, you cannot share data across directory trees. Parts of an object cannot exist in more than one directory tree. Each tree has its own database of objects, and that database is not visible from one tree to another. Be cognizant of this limitation before you create multiple trees.

Think small. A small directory tree should consist of an Organization container and two Organizational Unit containers, which can hold all the objects on the network. For example:

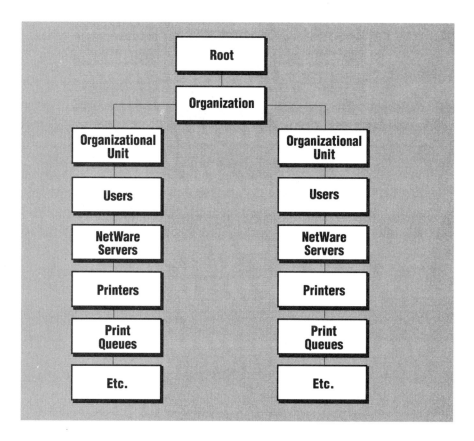

The easiest way to create your directory tree is to take a copy of the company's organizational chart and work from it—coming up with something similar to the following:

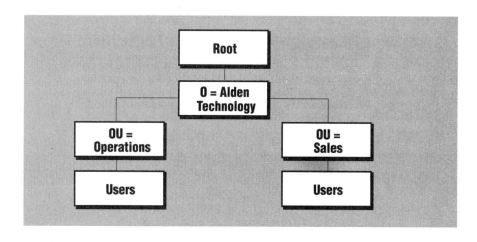

Look for other possible divisions. In addition to the organizational chart model, you can designate geographical locations, projects, products and so on.

More servers can be added in the future. As your network grows, you can install 4.0 on additional servers and add more Organization and Organizational Unit containers as needed.

For a large network that is composed of numerous servers, add more Organization and Organizational Unit containers, similar to the following:

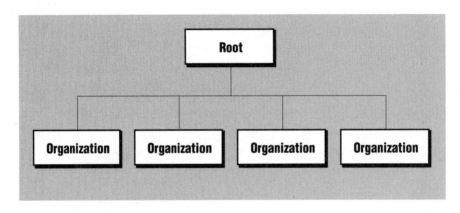

Following is an example:

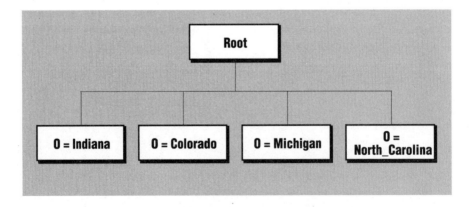

A disadvantage to creating more levels is that users' contexts become longer. As they become longer, they are more difficult to remember and, therefore, more difficult to use.

Leaf objects follow Organizational Objects. In the Organization and Organizational Unit container objects, there exist other objects that are end products, or leaf, objects. You can create the following leaf objects:

AFP Server	Print Queue
Alias	Print Server
Computer	Printer
Directory Map	Profile
Group	User
NetWare Server	Volume
Organizational Role	

Key leaf objects are created at installation. Default leaf objects, which are always created upon installation, are the NetWare server, Volume SYS, user ADMIN and user object Supervisor for bindery emulation on non-4.0 servers only. All others that are needed must be added.

ADMIN has full rights. User ADMIN has all rights to objects in the directory tree, and has Supervisor object rights to the NetWare server, rights to browse at the root, and Read and File Scan rights to SYS:PUBLIC. It is a good idea to change the ADMIN password as soon as possible after the installation is complete.

Servers are divided into one or more of the following:

■ *Volumes*, which are then divided into one or more directories.

- *Directories*, which contain subdirectories or files.

- *Subdirectories or files.*

OBJECT & PROPERTY RIGHTS

To view all the files on a volume, you must have the proper permissions. There are two types of permissions regarding directory listings: *object rights* and *property rights*. The object rights are for the directory only and have no bearing on individual files. Property rights, on the other hand, exist for each of the individual files. This ability to grant rights at the file level is new with version 4.0.

Following are the five different object rights:

- *Supervisor.* Essentially has all rights.

- *Browse.* Can see the names of all files.

- *Create.* Can make new files.

- *Delete.* Can remove existing files.

- *Rename.* Can change the existing name of a file to a new name.

Following are the five different property rights:

- *Supervisor.* Once again, essentially has all rights.

- *Compare.* Can compare objects to see whether a match is true or false.

- *Read.* Can read the files.

- *Write.* Can change the contents of files.

- *Add.* Can change the property rights to the file.

Create directories according to backup needs. You may not always need to back up the .EXE files, but you will always need to back up the database files that are constantly being modified. Keep directories holding data files apart from those that hold executables; this way, you don't have to wade through the directory, ignoring files that do not change to find the ones that do.

Keep DOS files in DOS volumes, Macintosh files in Mac volumes, UNIX files in UNIX volumes and so on. Because UNIX filenames can be 15 characters long, they take up more room in the File Allocation Table.

 Upon installation of the operating system, four directories are created by default. They are as follows:

- *SYS:LOGIN.* Holds files necessary for logging in.

- *SYS:MAIL.* Holds subdirectories that are created by the system for every user an administrator adds, and the one created automatically for ADMIN.

- *SYS:SYSTEM.* Holds the NetWare operating system and utilities.

- *SYS:PUBLIC.* Holds utilities for all users.

 Subdirectories can be created in various ways. You can create subdirectories using MD, MKDIR, the FILER menu or the NetWare Administrator utility.

 Keep operating systems on the server using the following convention:

```
SYS:PUBLIC/machine/os_type/os_version
```

For example, you might use the following:

```
SYS:PUBLIC/IBM_PC/MSDOS/5.0
```

Using this convention makes for uniformity across the network and across all networks if all administrators adhere to the same standard.

ATTRIBUTES

Directory and file attributes assign properties to a file reflecting the way it can be accessed. The attributes are assignable by the administrator or other users who have administrative rights. The following attributes apply to both files and directories:

DC	*Don't Compress.* This attribute overrides any attempt by the operating system for automatic compression.
DI	*Delete Inhibit.* The file cannot be deleted; this attribute overrides the erase trustee right.
DM	*Don't Migrate.* This attribute prevents the file\subdirectory from being moved from the server to other media (floppy, tape and so on).
H	*Hidden.* If you use this attribute, the user cannot see the file by using DIR but can by using NLIST if he or she has File Scan rights.
IC	*Immediate Compress.* With this attribute, the server can compress the file or subdirectory as soon as the file or subdirectory is closed by a user.
N	*Normal.* This attribute makes the files Read, Write and Nonshareable. It serves mostly as a timesaver, allowing you to specify one command instead of three.
P	*Purge.* This attribute erases a file as soon as it is deleted and prevents it from being unerased.
RI	*Rename Inhibit.* With this attribute, the file or subdirectory cannot be renamed.

SY	*SYstem attribute flag.* This attribute prevents the user from seeing the file by using DIR, but he or she can still see it by using NDIR or if he or she has File Scan rights.

The following attributes are for files only:

A	*Archive.* This attribute indicates the file has been changed since the last backup was performed.
CI	*Copy Inhibit.* This attribute prevents Macintosh users from copying files; it does not work with DOS or OS/2.
I	*Index.* With this attribute, the server can access large files more quickly via the FAT table.
RW	*Read and Write.* This attribute is the default setting for new files.
S	*Shareable.* If you add this attribute, more than one user can access the file.
T	*TTS (Transactional Tracking System).* If you add this attribute, the Transactional Tracking System is enabled.
X	*EXecute only.* If you use this attribute, the file cannot be copied, modified or backed up. The only way to change this attribute is to delete the file.

FLAG

You use the FLAG utility to show the current attributes of a file or change them to new values.

FLAG without any options shows the current attributes of a file. If you are uncertain as to what currently is assigned to the file, type FLAG and the filename to view.

Compress entire directories. To set all files in a directory to be compressed immediately each time they are closed, specify the directory and follow it with IC:

```
FLAG SYS:APPL\QA4\MEMOS IC
```

Prevent entire directories from being compressed. To keep files in the data directory from being compressed, use the DC option and follow it with /S to affect all subdirectories as well:

```
FLAG SYS:APPL\QA4\DATA DC /S
```

The attributes mentioned in the preceding section (DS, IC, etc.) are options that you can set using the FLAG command. In addition to these options, there are several others, which follow:

/D	Shows detailed information about the file or directory.
/DO	Shows directories only.
/FO	Shows files only.
/NAME I GROUP=name	Modifies the owner of a file or directory.

/M=mode	Modifies the search modes of executable files.
/S	Includes subdirectories.
/C	Continuously scrolls the output and does not pause for the user to press a key before continuing.
ALL	Assigns directories H, Sy, P, Di and Ri; or assigns files Ro, S, A, H, Sy, T, P, CI, DI and RI.

 You can set the following search modes for executable files:

0	(The default.) Looks for instructions in the NET.CFG file.
1	Searches the path specified in the file itself; if there is no path, searches the default directory and then looks in all search drives.
2	Searches the path specified in the file itself; if none, searches only default directory.
3	Searches the path specified in the file itself, the default directory, and then only if the open request is read does it search drives.
4	Reserved.

5	Searches the path specified, followed by all search drives, and if no paths are specified, then searches the default and all search drives.
6	Reserved.
7	Searches the specified path first; if an open request is read-only, then searches the search drives; if no path is defined, then searches the drives.

You also can use status flags for information only but cannot change them. As with other attributes, these are set by the administrator, or a user with administrative rights. They are as follows:

Cc	Can't compress
Co	Compressed
M	Migrated

RIGHTS

With RIGHTS, you can view or modify user or group rights for files, directories, subdirectories and volumes. The syntax for the command is as follows:

```
RIGHTS path [[+ | - ] rights] [/option]
```

Allowable options are as follows:

/F	Shows the Inherited Rights Filter.
GROUP=group name	Modifies rights for a group.
/INHERITED	Shows trustee and group rights that created the inherited rights or shows where they came from.
/SUB	Includes subdirectories.
/TRUSTEE	Shows trustees.
NAME=username	Modifies the rights for a user.
/C	Continuously scrolls the display and does not wait for the user to press a key to continue.
S	Assigns supervisory rights to the file.
R	Assigns read access to the file.
W	Grants write access to the file.
C	Assigns the ability to create files and subdirectories.
E	Grants rights to erase or delete files and subdirectories.
M	Modify.
F	File scan.
A	Access control.
N	No rights.

You can use wildcards with the RIGHTS command. One of the more commonly used is the one period (.), which stands for the current directory. For example, the following line gives read, write and create rights to the current subdirectory to all members of the support group:

```
RIGHTS . R W C /GROUP=SUPPORT
```

NDIR

Use the NDIR utility to view the following information about files:

- Dates
- Size
- Owner
- Attributes
- Archive bit

You also can use NDIR to view information on directories (and subdirectories as well), reporting the following:

- Creation date
- Owner
- Subdirectories
- Inherited rights mask
- Effective rights

You also can use NDIR to view information about the contents of volumes and sort the information for viewing.

The syntax for the command is as follows:

```
NDIR [filename] [option]
```

where available options are as follows:

/C	Continuously scrolls the display and does not prompt you to press a key for the next screen.
/CO	Shows only files and their compression sizes.
/DA	Displays when files were last updated, archived, accessed, created or copied.
/DE	Offers more specific DEtail.
/DO	Shows directories only.
/FI	Finds the location of specific FIles on all the available search drives.
/FO	Shows files only.
/LONG	Shows the long file names.
/MAC	Displays Macintosh files.
/R	Displays the inherited and effective rights.
/SORT AC	Sorts files by the date last accessed from the earliest to most recent.
/SORT AR	Sorts files by the date they were last archived from the earliest to the most recent.
/SORT CR	Shows files in order of creation or copy date from the earliest to the latest.

/SORT OW	Alphabetically sorts the display by file owner name.
/SORT SI	Shows the files in sorted order by size from the smallest file to the largest.
/SORT UP	Sorts files by the last update time from the earliest date or time to the latest.
/SORT UN	Suspends any sorting operations.
/SPA	Shows the volume SPAce limitation information.
/SUB	Shows SUBdirectories.
/VER	Gives VERsion information.
/VOL	Shows VOLumes.

 Attribute options apply. You also can specify files to list by any of the attribute options, such as A, CC, M and so on.

 Check deleted file status. To see a list of files that will be irretrievably removed upon deletion, use the P option.

 A rule of thumb. A slash (/) always precedes the first option of the option list, and a backslash (\) always goes before path names.

 Multiple options and wildcards are allowed. You must separate multiple options by spaces. NDIR fully supports wildcards.

Look for hidden files. Use NDIR K: FO H to show all hidden files in the K: directory.

 You can check available disk space using NDIR and check multiple volumes with the following syntax:

```
NDIR {volume to check}: /VOL
```

MOVING ON

In this chapter, you learned how to establish a directory tree, list files and view the attributes assigned to them. With this information, you also know how to change those attributes to make them reflect the environment you want.

Although it would be wonderful if files could exist only on hard drives, alas it is not true. The majority of the time, you must generate a hard copy of them in some form. Chapter 6, "Printer Enchantment," discusses how to set up print devices and print files to them.

Chapter 6

PRINTER ENCHANTMENT

In the preceding chapter, you learned that networks evolved for two real reasons: to share information and to share printers. The only thing that has changed is that printers have become more expensive, office space has become more valuable, and now more than ever the need for sharing printers with all users on the network is prevalent.

NetWare 4.0 changed the printing setup so that now users can send print jobs to an individual printer and not to a print queue, as was done in the past. NetWare fulfills the desired function by utilizing a print queue, print server and printer driver to allow several network workstations to print to the same printer and save the cost of expensive hardware.

Although users can now address printers directly, it is still true that when a user sends a print job from a workstation, NetWare temporarily stores the job in a network directory called a print queue until the server can relay the job to a printer. In release 4.0, the print queue is in the QUEUES subdirectory at the root of the selected volume, as opposed to bindery-based systems, which use the SYS:SYSTEM subdirectory.

The purpose of the print server is to monitor queues and printers. It takes print jobs from the queue and sends them to the assigned printer. A definable option determines how often the queue is examined for spooled jobs, with the default being every 15 seconds.

A print server is a station loaded with PSERVER.NLM, which will support between 1 and 256 printers. The printers can attach directly to the network, to print servers or to network workstations.

Additionally, you can load the printer driver, NPRINTER, as an NLM at any server or as an EXE on any workstation to turn the printer attached to it into a network printer.

 Don't forget a PostScript printer. If you intend to print any of the NetWare manual, you will need one.

SETTING UP PRINTING OPERATIONS

One of the most difficult peripherals to configure is a printer. You can put a network together and have the server and all workstations talking within a matter of hours and then spend weeks trying to get the printers to function properly. Printers are made with so many configurable options that the number of setups possible with one printer is mind-boggling. On the plus side, however, once you get a printer functioning properly, it will usually stay that way for a very long time.

 Good news for those who upgrade. If you're upgrading from a previous version of NetWare, the existing printing environment carries over, and you don't need to re-create the setup.

 To see how to modify print services using Windows, check Chapter 8, "Windows Marvels." The rest of this chapter details how to modify the print services with the command line.

 After you get printers functioning properly, write down the configuration and tape it to their undersides. This way, when a printer needs to be serviced or replaced, you don't end up at square one again.

The easy way. The simplest network printing arrangement is a parallel printer cabled to the file server.

 If a printer functions properly in a non-networked environment, it will work in a networked environment with NetWare 4.0. Printers do not suffer from strokes and suddenly quit working because they are connected to networks. If a printer is not functioning on the network, take it off and see whether that isolates the problem; most of the time the answer is no.

 Follow this easy setup of one parallel printer off the server:

1. Connect the printer to the parallel port of the server.

2. Log in as ADMIN at a workstation and type **PSETUP**.

3. For default values, press F10. Pressing this function key creates a print server with the default name taken from the name of the server you logged into plus "_Print_Server." It also creates a printer with the default name of "PrinterName" and a print queue with the default name taken from the name of the printer plus "_Q."

   For example, if the server name is Alden, then the print server becomes Alden_Print_Server, the printer is Printer-Name, and the print queue becomes PrinterName_Q.

4. At the console, type **LOAD PSERVER Alden_Print_Server**.

5. Go for a carbonated beverage of your choice.

Name printers logically. It is a recommended practice to name printers and queues geographically for the benefit of users trying to figure out where their print jobs are going. For example, a printer located in the sales office can simply be named SALES.

Make certain you have sufficent disk space. Estimate 15 to 20 percent of the server disk space, on an average system, is used for spooling print queue jobs.

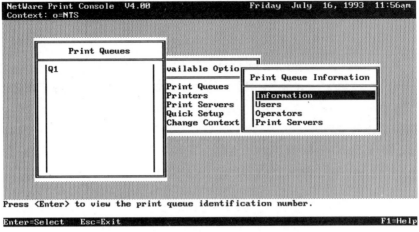

```
NetWare Print Console  V4.00              Friday  July  16, 1993  11:56am
Context: o=NTS


      ┌─────────────────────┐
      │     Print Queues     │
      │ ┌Q1                  ┌──vailable Optio┌────────────────────────────┐
      │ │                    │Print Queues    │ Print Queue Information     │
      │ │                    │Printers        ├────────────────────────────┤
      │ │                    │Print Servers   │Information                  │
      │ │                    │Quick Setup     │Users                        │
      │ │                    │Change Context  │Operators                    │
      │ │                                     │Print Servers                │
      │ │                                     └────────────────────────────┘
      │ │
      │ │
      │ │
      └─┴──────────────────┘

Press <Enter> to view the print queue identification number.

Enter=Select   Esc=Exit                                           F1=Help
```

Figure 6-1: NETUSER lets users view their printer connections.

PRINTING UTILITIES

Ten utilities relate to printing. In alphabetic order, they are:

■ *CAPTURE*. Redirects output from a workstation's printer to the network.

■ *NETUSER*. Captures output, prints files from outside applications and monitors print queues. It also sends, modifies or deletes print jobs.

■ *NPRINT*. Prints files from outside applications.

■ *NPRINTER*. Allows network access to network printers— NLM on the server, EXE on workstations.

■ *PCONSOLE*. Monitors, creates and modifies print queues, servers and printers. Also sends, modifies or deletes print jobs.

■ *PRINTCON*. Simplifies NPRINT and CAPTURE commands by creating print job configurations.

■ *PRINTDEF*. Defines print devices and forms to create a database for use in PRINTCON.

■ *PSC*. Allows you to view printer and printer status from the command line.

- *PSERVER.* Acts as print server software—NLM on the server.

- *PSETUP.* Creates and modifies print servers and printers. Automatically creates a queue for each printer by adding _Q to printer name.

CAPTURE

You use CAPTURE to print to a network printer what was originally intended for a local printer. You also can use this utility to print screen displays and save data to a network file. The options it supports are as follows:

SH	SHow; views the current status of LPT ports.
Server=NetWareserver	Indicates to which non-4.0 server the print job should be sent; the default is the current server.
Printer=printername	Tells to which printer to send the job; the default is in PRINTCON.
Queue=printqueuename	Specifies to which print queue to send the job.
Endcap or EndCap CAncel	Ends the capturing of print jobs and lets them go to the LPT ports once more. The CAncel also cancels any jobs that are spooled to print now.
CReate=path	Creates a text file in which to store printed data.

ALL	Used with Endcap; ends the capture of all LPT ports at once.
LPT=(1–3)	Indicates which port to capture.
Job=jobname	Specifies which PRINTCON job configuration this print job is to use.
Verbose	Allows you to view more detailed information about the printer, queue, etc., than is shown with SHow.
Keep	If a workstation fails, captured data is kept in the print queue.
No Banner	Does not print usual one-page banner before a print job, telling who requested it and when.
Banner=banner name	Allows you to specify up to 12 characters to appear in the lower half of the banner page.
NAMe=user name	Allows you to specify up to 12 characters to appear in the upper half of the banner page.
/Form=formname	Specifies the form name or number the printer will use.
/Copies=n	Tells how many copies of the document to print; the default is 1 but can be any number up to 255.

Tabs=n	Tells how many spaces a tab is to equal; the default is 1 but can be any number up to 18.
/No Tabs	Cancels existing tab settings.
/TImeout=n	Tells how many seconds should elapse before closing a print job after the last data is received; can be any number from 0 to 1000.
/Form Feed	Sends a blank page at the end of the print job.
/No Form Feed	Does not send a blank page at the end of a print job.
/AUtoend	Specifies the captured data be closed and sent to the printer after exiting an application.
/No Autoend	Specifies that the captured data is not closed and sent to the printer after exiting an application.
/NOTIfy	Tells the user when the print job is finished printing.
/No NOTIfy	Does not tell the user when a print job is finished printing.

All captures are transitory. The capturing and rerouting of the local printer port is a temporary capability that is lost with each power-down of the workstation. For CAPTURE to take effect, you must reset it on each reboot. The most effective solution to this problem is to place the CAPTURE command inside login scripts.

The defaults include a banner page, auto endcap, no tabs and form feed. Be sure to override them if you don't want them active. The most common overrides are /NB and /NFF to cancel the wasted banner page and the form feed at the end of the print job.

 CAPTURE can redirect only LPT ports. You cannot specify the capture of a COM port.

Check the status. If you're requesting print jobs over and over, and nothing is printing out, use CAPTURE /SH to verify that an application has not canceled your network printing.

Check the workstation ports. To see what LPT ports exist on a workstation, you can use the MSD command if you're running MS-DOS 6.0 on the workstation. You then see the Microsoft diagnostic screen, which shows the configuration of the workstation, including the number of parallel and serial ports.

If you don't have MS-DOS 6.0 running, you can type **DEBUG** at a command line and then enter the following:

```
D40:0000
```

An eight-line display will appear, showing hexadecimal entries on the left and ASCII on the right. The first line is all that you are interested in, and it will look similar to the following:

```
F8 03 F8 02 00 00 00 00-78 03 BC 03 BC 03 00 00
```

The number of F8s indicate the number of serial ports in the workstation, while the characters to the right of the dash show the number of LPT, or parallel, ports. Each port is represented by two sets of numbers; thus, in this example, there are three parallel ports. In the following example, there is only one:

```
F8 03 F8 02 00 00 00 00-78 02 00 00 00 00 00 00
```

Type **q** and press Enter at a blank line to exit the DEBUG utility and return to a prompt.

Be cognizant of other applications. If DesqView is running on the workstation, the number of parallel ports shown will be correct, but no serial ports will be shown (the values will all be zeros). Exit from DesqView and run DEBUG again to get a true reading.

NETUSER

NETUSER lets you manage objects. It is discussed in Chapter 2, "Menu Magic."

NPRINT

NPRINT prints ASCII files or files already formatted for a printer. The syntax is as follows:

```
NPRINT filename options
```

where allowable options are as follows:

Server=NetWareserver	Indicates to which non-4.0 server the print job should be sent; the default is the current server.
Printer=printername	Tells to which printer to send the job; the default is in PRINTCON.
Queue=printqueuename	Specifies to which print queue to send the job.
ALL	Used with Endcap to end the capture of all LPT ports at once.
LPT=(1–3)	Indicates which port to capture.

Job=jobname	Specifies which PRINTCON job configuration this print job is to use.
Verbose	Allows you to view more detailed information about the printer, queue, etc., than is shown with SHow.
No Banner	Does not print usual one-page banner before a print job, telling who requested it and when.
Banner=banner name	Allows you to specify up to 12 characters to appear in the lower half of the banner page.
NAMe=user name	Allows you to specify up to 12 characters to appear in the upper half of the banner page.
/Form=formname	Specifies the form name or number the printer will use.
/Copies=n	Tells how many copies of the document to print; the default is 1 but can be any number up to 65000.
Tabs=n	Tells how many spaces a tab is to equal; the default is 1 but can be any number up to 18.
/No Tabs	Cancels existing tab settings.
/Form Feed	Sends a blank page at the end of the print job.

/No Form Feed	Does not send a blank page at the end of a print job.
/NOTIfy	Tells the user when the print job is finished printing.
/No NOTIfy	Does not tell the user when a print job is finished printing.

 Defaults exist. As with CAPTURE, defaults for NPRINT are for a banner page, automatic endcap, no tabs and a form feed.

 NPRINT works only with LPT ports. Serial ports cannot be printed to.

 NPRINT is resident in active memory. NPRINT is not a Terminate-and-Stay-Resident (TSR) program, like the MS-DOS PRINT utility.

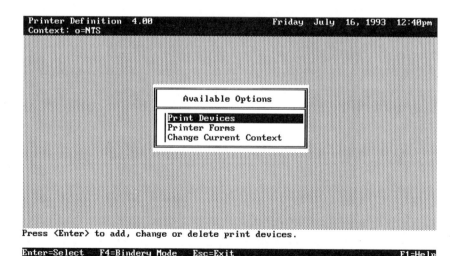

Figure 6-2: A NetWare 4.0 network administrator who prefers a GUI to command-line functions can view and manage print job configurations through NETADMIN.

NPRINTER

The NPRINTER utility is a new addition to NetWare. With it, you can attach network printers directly to a server without running a separate print server (PSERVER). You can load multiple NPRINTER.NLMs on a server. To do so, go to the console, and type the following at the colon prompt:

```
LOAD NPRINTER PRINTERNAME
```

 NPRINTER can appear on every boot. If you want NPRINTER to come up every time you boot, load the above commands (LOAD NPRINTER PRINTERNAME) in the AUTOEXEC.NCF file.

If NPRINTER is to run on a workstation, it needs access to six files: NPRINTER.EXE, NPRINTER.MSG, NPRINTER.HEP, SYS$MSG.MSG, SYS$HELP.HEP and IBM$RUN.

The NPRINTER command syntax that existed in previous versions is still supported:

```
NPRINTER Printservername Printernumber
```

as well as the new syntax:

```
Load NPRINTER Printername
```

PCONSOLE

Using PCONSOLE, you can manage print queue, server and printer objects in the way NETUSER manages users.

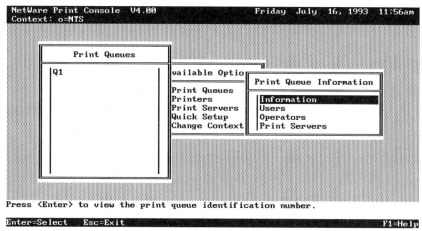

Figure 6-3: PCONSOLE lets a 4.0 administrator manage objects that relate to network printing functions.

PRINTCON

Using the PRINTCON utility, you can set your current directory path; modify, view or add print job configurations; and specify what print job configuration will be used when one is not specified with CAPTURE, NPRINT or PCONSOLE.

PRINTDEF

You use the PRINTDEF utility to define devices in a database that become the input for PRINTCON. It is a menu utility used exclusively for defining printers and control codes.

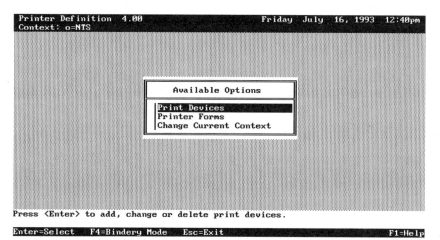

Figure 6-4: The PRINTDEF utility lets a 4.0 administrator define printers and control codes.

PSC

PSC controls the print servers and network printers from the command line. You can use the following options:

ABort	Aborts a printer.
CancelDown	Cancels bringing down the print server.
FormFeed	Sends a blank page at the end of a print job.
MARK {char}	Marks the top of the form on the printer with a character; the default character is the asterisk (*).
MOunt Form=n	Indicates the form number for the printer to use.
Pause	Pauses the printer.
Print Server=printserver	
Printer=printernumber	
PRIvate	Prevents users from using a printer on your workstation until you release it.
Server=NetWareservername	
SHAred	Cancels the PRIvate command.
STARt	Starts a printer.
STATus	Indicates the status of the printer.
STOp	Stops a printer.

PSETUP

You can use the PSETUP utility—in addition to creating print services, as was done in the "Setting Up Printing Operations" section—to modify multiple printers and print servers. It also allows you to do the following:

- Change the current NetWare server or view attached servers.

- Show the number of printers defined on the current server.

- View, add or remove printers.

- Describe a printer with details.

- Set a printer type and port.

- Indicate whether the printer attaches to a workstation or server.

- Indicate the interrupt the printer will use.

 To rename or change the print queue and printer assignments, follow these steps:

1. Connect the parallel or serial printer to the server or workstation.

2. Log in as ADMIN on a workstation and type **PSETUP**.

3. Follow the instructions at the bottom of the screen to do the following:

   Add or delete printers.

   Modify the printer name, type and settings.

   Add or delete print servers.

   Change the print server name.

   Change the current NetWare server or context.

PSERVER

PSERVER is the print server utility that must be running before print jobs move from their queues to printers.

Workstations or servers can print only after you load a print server in one of the following ways:

- PSERVER.NLM on the server.

- PSERVER.EXE on the workstation.

 A print server is a software program that monitors printers and print queues—PSERVER.NLM or .EXE. Think of it as the watchdog of all printing processes. Because one can handle up to 256 printers, you should not need more than one print server for every NetWare server.

Novell recommends that you run PSERVER.NLM on the server and not on workstations. When run on a workstation, PSERVER.NLM prevents that connection from doing anything else, whereas when you run it on the server, the server is still fully functional.

If you do need more than 256 printers on the network, the recommendation is to load the first batch on the server and then load the additional printers on another server or a dedicated workstation.

Setup is read-only at start-up. If a print server is running, you must take it down and bring it back up before it will recognize any changes that you've made in the setup.

If you're running PSERVER.EXE on a workstation, edit the NET.CFG on that machine and enter the following line:

```
SPX Connection=nn
```

where *nn* is twice the number of printers that will be running from the workstation.

For the print server to run on a workstation, that workstation must have access to six key files: PSERVER.EXE, PSERVER.MSG, PSERVER.HEP, SYS$MSG.MSG, SYS$HELP.HEP and IBM$RUN.OVL.

SERIAL vs. PARALLEL

Use parallel printers whenever possible. Although the distance they offer is not as great as with serial printers, they reduce the risk of printing problems.

Electrical interference can interrupt print jobs if the cable is too long or susceptible to electrical noise. Fluorescent lights are the worst source of electrical noise and can severely corrupt what appears on a serial printer.

Parallel printing is four to six times faster than serial, and the hardware is universal. With serial printers, in addition to being slower, the pins within the cable must be crossed and set.

The recommended distance of a parallel cable is only 10 feet. With extenders, you can occasionally bump this number up to as much as 150 feet, at which time the parallel cable becomes as susceptible to noise as serial, if not more.

Serial cables have greater length. As opposed to parallel, they usually start at 25 feet long and can go up to 250 or even 500 feet in length.

With serial printers, you need a 25-pin to 9-pin adapter. With serial printers, most parameters default to common settings: polled interrupt, no X-ON/X-OFF, no parity, 9600 baud, 8 data bits and 1 stop bit.

Serial printers allow for configurable X-ON/X-OFF options. When X-ON/X-OFF is enabled, the software does the error checking, and when it is disabled, the hardware does the error checking.

Serial interfaces are not meant for printers. Serial printers use RS232-C cable and an interface that was developed for terminal-to-modem communications. You must trick the serial ports into thinking they are communicating with Data Communications Equipment (DCE) on the other side.

TROUBLESHOOTING

 If you cannot get a workstation printer to print, make sure the following line is not in NET.CFG:

```
LOCAL PRINTERS=0
```

If this line is present, delete it or make the number of printers equal to 1 or the number of printers you have on the workstation.

Corrupted print jobs. If you have corrupted print jobs, un-known queue errors, errors when trying to access a queue or a prompt for a password when the print server is loaded, then delete print queues and the print server and add them again. Their descriptions have become corrupted.

Nothing printing. If an application says a print job was sent, yet nothing prints out, check to see if CAPTURE was used before you began the application. If it was, use PCONSOLE to see if anything is spooling up or waiting on a printer.

Safeguard the printer. To keep a printer working for a long time, ventilate the area around the printer as well as you can, and keep the printer itself clean. The more you can do this, the longer you will get high-quality print output.

Remember not to have the ventilation of laser printers aimed at people or desks. A high amount of electronic radiation is created in the process of laser printing, and the fans should be blowing away from people.

Read the instructions. There is a purpose for those that came with your printer. Read them and follow the manufacturer's recommendations for maintaining the printer.

 Get the right printer drivers to do the jobs requested. You cannot use a Phillips screwdriver to take out headlights that were put in a car with a Torx wrench. By the same token, you cannot expect a printer to do a job for which it does not have the tools.

Chunk printing. If high-resolution graphics are printing out in chunks and getting interrupted by other print jobs, increase the printing timeout values by using CAPTURE. When the application is waiting too long to send the next packet, NetWare acts as though the request is done.

Use CAPTURE Sh to show what the timeout is. You can increase the number of seconds or disable the timeout altogether by using CAPTURE TI=0.

Large jobs spool for a long time. Bear in mind that graphic images naturally take longer to go across the network to a spooler than if they were printing locally. If it is at all feasible to print these jobs locally, by all means do so.

MOVING ON

In this chapter, you learned about printing and its various aspects. You can connect printers to the server or to workstations, and you can send print jobs to print queues or directly to printers called by name—a new feature of release 4.0.

Chapter 7, "Workstation Wonders," follows, and in it we will discuss the optimal setup for a workstation, bearing in mind that quantity-wise, workstations outnumber all other components of the network. In addition to covering various versions of workstation operating systems, including MS-DOS and DR DOS, we will also go over diskless workstations and utilities that can make managing them an easier task. Read on....

Chapter 7

WORKSTATION WONDERS

The server holds information pertinent to users on the network, and the NetWare operating system is responsible for ensuring that the server can disseminate that information to users who request it. Workstations, in their barest sense, are the means by which the users receive and process their packets of information.

You can spend your money buying the latest operating system and the fastest server imaginable, but users are still limited by the speed and capability of the workstation they're using. All components must work together and operate at maximum efficiency if the network is expected to do the work at peak capacity.

In this chapter, we will look at ways of making workstations competitive components of the network and not merely the slow-footed means by which information trickles from server to user.

CHOOSING THE RIGHT OPERATING SYSTEM

The majority of all NetWare workstations run on one of three operating systems: OS/2, MS-DOS or DR DOS (also known as Novell DOS). OS/2 is far and away the underdog in terms of number of copies installed, thus for simplicity's sake we will focus on the two DOS systems. Novell's entry will be referred to throughout the rest of this chapter as DR DOS simply because all versions prior to 7.0 have gone under that title.

 If you're not running the latest release of your operating system, upgrade it. Every release offers new features not previously available. These features are intended to increase the productivity of the operating system. Bear in mind, the more productive the workstation operating system is, the faster it can handle requests, and the faster it can communicate with the network.

At the very least, all MS-DOS workstations should be running version 5.0, and 6.0 is highly recommended. If you still have versions 3.3 or 4.0 floating around, you're wasting valuable resources. At the very least, all DR DOS workstations should be running version 6.0.

Novell recommends that you store DOS versions in the following directory:

```
SYS:PROGRAMS\DOS\%OS_VERSION
```

Using this directory creates uniformity across networks.

DR DOS 6.0, however, does not return version 6.00 from the %OS_VERSION variable mentioned in the preceding tip. Instead it returns version 3.31.

Either operating system—MS-DOS or DR DOS—will work perfectly well in a NetWare environment. Each operating system offers benefits that the other does not have, while both perform the same basic functions. MS-DOS is marketed by the premier PC operating system supplier, whereas DR DOS is marketed by the premier network operating system manufacturer. It is six points in favor of one operating system and half a dozen for the other. Which one you choose to use will have minimal effect on the large picture and affect only the options available on the individual workstation.

The following tips compare the benefits each system offers over the other. Again, none of these differences are crucial but instead should be looked upon as supplemental.

With version 6.0, Microsoft included DBLSPACE. This is an internal answer to the success of third-party disk compression utilities. This same feature is available with DR DOS by using the SUPERSTOR utility licensed from AddStor and included with the operating system.

Workstation compression utilities reduce the cost of increasing the hard drive capacity, and you can think of them as an inexpensive alternative to hardware upgrades. Compressing the disk on the workstation works the same way as it does on the server: by making individual files smaller, you increase the capacity of the hard drive. In this manner, a 40mb hard drive has the same storage capacity as an 80mb hard drive; an 80mb hard drive has the same capacity as a 160mb hard drive and so on.

Anti-virus protection is available in MS-DOS. Version 6.0 provides this via MSAV—a virus-scanning utility licensed from Central Point Software. If you're running DR DOS, splurge a few bucks and buy a copy of a good virus-detection routine. Install it on workstations, and encourage users to utilize it.

You can preach for a month of Sundays to users about how they should not bring in disks from Aunt Edna's cousin Landon, who dials into bulletin boards and was once investigated by the House Committee on Anti-American Activities, but you know that they're still going to do it. Landon is going to show them a clever screen-blanking routine called Road-Kill Weekend, and they are just going to have to have a copy of it on their workstations at the office. After all, what's the harm?

The harm is that the workstation is connected to a network, and if Road-Kill Weekend contains a virus, that virus may traverse the network wire and infect every workstation on the network, not to mention the server. Instead of sermonizing about not bringing contraband programs into the office, give users the ability to scan the programs they do bring in and encourage them to do so, as well as scan their entire system on a regular basis.

DR DOS, as opposed to MS-DOS, is available in a LAN Pack version. This makes it possible for you to install the software on a workstation directly from the server. Installing from the server saves time if you have 100 workstations and want all to be on the same operating version but don't have the time to visit each one individually.

Using DR DOS, you can assign passwords to files and directories as well as globally on the local hard drive. If you leave the workstation for a while, you can lock the screen and require someone to give a password before allowing access. These features are missing in MS-DOS.

Following is a key feature-by-feature comparison of DOS version 6.0 for each vendor. Novell DOS 7.0 includes peer-to-peer networking capabilities and enhanced security features.

Feature	DR DOS 6	MS-DOS 6
Ability to assign passwords	yes	no
Anti-virus protection included	no	yes
Built-in defragmenter	yes	yes
Command-line history and recall	yes	yes
Full-screen ASCII editor	yes	yes
Hard disk compression	yes	yes
Interactive prompt in batch files	yes	yes

Feature	DR DOS 6	MS-DOS 6
Link laptops & portables to PCs	yes	yes
MOVE command	yes	yes
Online documentation	yes	yes
Recursive delete capabilities	yes	yes
Undelete files	yes	yes
Upper memory manager included	yes	yes
Windows compatible	yes	yes

OPTIMIZING FOR MAXIMUM PERFORMANCE

You can optimize workstations, like servers, to run at their highest performance levels. Because, as mentioned earlier in this book, I am assuming you're running NetWare 4.0, I also must assume that we are not talking about a network with three workstations but instead one with 100 or more.

When we discuss those numbers, you can see that it is impractical for one person to be responsible for overseeing the day-to-day operation of every workstation. Instead, you should give users the responsibility of maintaining their own workstations and verifying that all is running as smoothly as possible—limited empowerment, if you will.

You should make each user responsible for his or her own backup, virus scan and optimization, among other things. When the user encounters difficulties, then he or she should summon the system administrator, but the system administrator's time is too valuable to be wasted on tasks that can be assigned locally. For that reason, I encourage you to encourage users to use the following tips.

Use memory optimization. Both DOS operating systems include memory optimization programs that load as many device drivers as possible into the upper memory area normally set aside for hardware expansion cards. By optimizing memory, more of the lower memory is available for application software. Because most application software can use only lower memory, this feature serves as a definite benefit.

 Use file-defragmenting utilities on a regular basis. When a file fills an allocation block, it then begins to use another block. If the next block is not available, the file must go to the next available one and begin writing there. When you read the file back in, the drive heads must skip around on the drive to find all blocks that contain portions of the file.

File defragmenters place all the blocks that contain portions of a file in consecutive order on the disk. In this manner, read and write time is increased—the amount of time depends on how fragmented the file and the disk were. Both operating systems offer defragmenting utilities with their latest releases. Persuade users to run the utility approximately once a month, and the speed of accessing files on their local drives will never lag too much.

Be forewarned, defragmenting compressed drives takes considerably longer than defragmenting uncompressed counterparts. The files must be uncompressed in memory before they can be defragmented and then recompressed once more. You might stress to users that 4:45 p.m. on Friday is not a good time to think about defragmenting the local hard drive.

 Keep PATH statements as short as possible. The longer the PATH statement, the more subdirectories that have to be searched when invalid commands are given.

 Use shortcut commands whenever possible. For example, the following command gives a list showing only subdirectories:

```
DIR ...
```

A great many tricks can help you operate more efficiently within the DOS workstation environment, and it's worth the time it takes to review them every once in a while.

Voodoo DOS is a good source of workstation command tips, and several other books that also serve this purpose are available.

Memory caches speed the performance of servers, and they do the same for workstations. On a workstation, a cache stores information that is read in from the local drive. If that information is needed again, it can be retrieved from the cache, rather than having to be read from the disk again. The difference in access time is incomparable, with cache memory winning hands down every time.

To increase workstation speed, consider adding RAM and installing cache software before you consider upgrading the processor.

Many utilities spool print jobs and allow a user to get back to work more quickly. In the preceding chapter, "Printer Enchantment," you learned how NetWare spools print jobs and then begins printing them.

If you have a spooler installed on the local workstation, it feeds the print request into it—which takes a set amount of time—and then lets the user go back to work. In the background, the spooler then sends the request to NetWare, which starts spooling it up. Basically, you have two spoolers running, and each one waits until it receives the whole packet before doing anything else. In other words, you're actually defeating the purpose and slowing printing down by having a spooler running locally.

DISKLESS WORKSTATIONS

The only real purpose for using diskless workstations is to increase network security. They are somewhat cheaper than regular workstations but usually not enough to justify their existence on a cost basis. They are almost impossible to upgrade and usually feature built-in interfaces that can never be upgraded.

Diskless workstations are totally useless when the network goes down because there is no local drive for the user to flounder on for a while. And in case you weren't reading the past few sentences carefully, I am not a big proponent of diskless workstations.

If you have diskless workstations, users cannot take their work home with them. If a report must be done Monday morning, it matters little that the company had an incentive program and helped users buy PCs for their homes. If that report is going to be done on Monday, someone has to let Young Johnny Beancounter in the office on Saturday so he can access the network and write the provocative study on paperclip usage that will reshape the way we all live and breathe.

Think of psychological effects. There is no quicker way to make employees feel untrusted than to give them a workstation without a hard drive or even a floppy disk drive. This situation is kind of like giving them a parking spot right by the door but not letting them drive to work because you're afraid they might scrape against the company president's car.

You can deal with security issues in many ways, including passwords, attributes, trustees, groups and so on. In my opinion, banning drives should be placed low on the list.

Many programs, including Windows, need temporary directories where they store work that is in progress. With diskless workstations, these temporary directories have to exist on the file server. This situation increases the network traffic, slows the speed of the workstation and increases the likelihood of slowing down other users.

Look for regular workstations that have been limited. A few vendors market diskless workstations that are nothing more than regular workstations that have been modified to boot without drives. Consider purchasing these over true diskless workstations, and if you ever have to convert them to regular workstations, you can do so fairly easily.

For diskless workstations to boot, you first must create a remote boot image file. It exists as NET$DOS.SYS in the SYS:LOGIN directory.

To create the remote boot image file, follow these steps:

1. Boot a workstation and log in as supervisor.

2. Map drive F: to SYS:SYSTEM.

3. Map drive G: to SYS:LOGIN.

4. Change to drive G:.

5. Run DOSGEN.

6. Copy an AUTOEXEC.BAT file into the SYS:LOGIN directory.

7. Flag the file shareable with the following command:

   ```
   Flag NET$DOS.SYS S
   ```

8. Grant the Modify right to the remote user in SYS:LOGIN:

   ```
   GRANT M TO MADONNA
   ```

UTILITIES & TOOLS

Utilities and tools help you increase the efficiency of a workstation or recover from a disaster. They fall into the two categories of maintenance and recovery.

 Keep a copy of the Norton Utilities handy. As operating systems have evolved, they have come to incorporate many of the utilities that used to be available only in third-party packages. Norton's is one of the few packages that have continued to evolve with the times and offer options still not available in the operating systems.

The latest version, 7.0, has the ability to recover damaged files that have been compressed as well as corrupted application files, including dBASE, Clipper, Lotus and WordPerfect. You also can encrypt files with password protection, sort directories and search through all files for specific text or information.

Never overlook the tools that come with the operating system.
These tools include the defragment utilities mentioned earlier in this chapter and MSD, the Microsoft Diagnostic tool that tells what components are found connected to the workstation's board.

You should also be familiar with as many facets of existing commands as possible. For example, to alphabetize directory listings, include the following command in the AUTOEXEC.BAT file:

```
SET DIRCMD=/O:N
```

All files will then be shown in alphabetic order anytime a user types the DIR command.

 If you have time to learn just one operating system utility in MS-DOS, make it DOSKEY. This macro utility will allow you to customize your operating system to meet your individual needs.

 REMOTE CONSOLE, a utility included with NetWare, lets you manage servers from a workstation on a network or via a modem. You can use console commands at the workstation as if you were actually at the console. Other things you can do include the following:

- Scan directories and edit text files.
- Transfer files to, but not from, the server.
- Bring down the server or reboot it.
- Install or upgrade NetWare on a remote server.

To run the utility across a modem, you need a workstation that has a modem, quite naturally, and it must be a 386 or 486 with 48k of available memory. When you're running the utility from a workstation on the network, you need only a PC with DOS 2.x or greater and 200k of available memory.

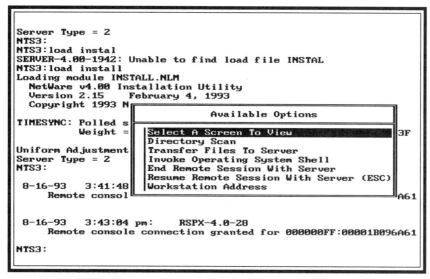

```
Server Type = 2
NTS3:
NTS3:load instal
SERVER-4.00-1942: Unable to find load file INSTAL
NTS3:load install
Loading module INSTALL.NLM
  NetWare v4.00 Installation Utility
  Version 2.15    February 4, 1993
  Copyright 1993 N┌──────────────────────────────────────────┐
                  │           Available Options                │
TIMESYNC: Polled s│┌──────────────────────────────────────────┐
           Weight =││Select A Screen To View                  ││3F
                   ││Directory Scan                           ││
Uniform Adjustment ││Transfer Files To Server                 ││
Server Type = 2    ││Invoke Operating System Shell            ││
NTS3:              ││End Remote Session With Server            ││
                   ││Resume Remote Session With Server (ESC)  ││
  8-16-93   3:41:48││Workstation Address                      ││
      Remote consol│└──────────────────────────────────────────┘A61

  8-16-93   3:43:04 pm:    RSPX-4.0-28
     Remote console connection granted for 000000FF:00001B096A61

NTS3:
```

Figure 7-1: RCONSOLE, or Remote Console, lets you use a network workstation or a remote workstation across a modem to manage a server.

To run the utility, go to the server and type the following at the colon prompt:

```
LOAD REMOTE [password]
```

Next, go to the workstation and type the following line at the command-line prompt:

```
LOAD RSPX
```

And you are up and running as if at the console. You must match the password that was typed on the console, and you will be prompted for it. Following are the active function keys:

F1	Provides help.
Alt-F1	Accesses the REMOTE CONSOLE menu.
Alt-F2	Exits REMOTE CONSOLE.
Alt-F3	Cycles backward through current screens.
Alt-F4	Cycles forward through current screens.
Alt-F5	Shows the address of the workstation you're using.

Use NETUSER. NETUSER, discussed in Chapter 2, "Menu Magic," is one of the most helpful menu utilities because it combines features of other command-line or menu utilities.

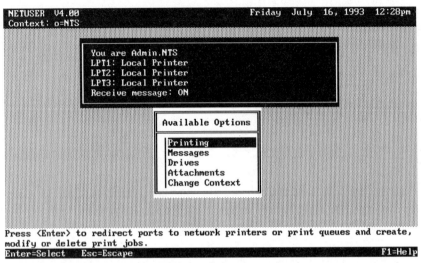

```
NETUSER  V4.00                            Friday  July  16, 1993  12:28pm
Context: o=NTS


            ┌─────────────────────────────────────┐
            │ You are Admin.NTS                    │
            │ LPT1: Local Printer                  │
            │ LPT2: Local Printer                  │
            │ LPT3: Local Printer                  │
            │ Receive message: ON                  │
            └─────────────────────────────────────┘

                   ┌──Available Options──┐
                   │ Printing            │
                   │ Messages            │
                   │ Drives              │
                   │ Attachments         │
                   │ Change Context      │
                   └─────────────────────┘



 Press <Enter> to redirect ports to network printers or print queues and create,
 modify or delete print jobs.
 Enter=Select   Esc=Escape                                          F1=Help
```

Figure 7-2: NETUSER lets a NetWare 4.0 user perform functions that in earlier versions required several command-line or menu utilities.

Become familiar with TSA. The DOS Workstation Target Service Agent (DOS TSA) gives Storage Management Engines the capability to access a DOS workstation's local drive for backup and restore operations. It offers several levels of security and an optional switch that will automatically attempt to reconnect if the existing connection is broken.

As a TSR, it runs in the background and occupies less than 7k of memory. All that is required to run it is MS-DOS 3.2 and higher, or DR DOS 5.0 and higher.

The syntax for the command is as follows:

```
TSA-DOS [ parameters ]
```

where available parameters are as follows:

/d	Drive.
/se	Server.
/t	Trust; allows the system administrator access without a password.
/n	Workstation name; 10-character maximum.
/b	Buffer size; in kilobytes, ranging from 2 to 20.
/h	Help.
/p	Password.
/r	Reconnect.
/remove	Removes the program from memory.
/st	Stack size; the default is 1024 bytes, with a range of 512 to 2048.
/u	Unload TSA.

Specifying trust disables the default requirement for a password. Use it with caution.

The password will be echoed if you enter it on the command line. To avoid this situation, wait for NetWare to prompt you for the password.

 You can run TBM12 before you run MS-DOS DOSSHELL or DR DOS TASKMAX to create an environment for multitasking. DesqView or Windows are better choices, but if they are not available, TMB12 is a good utility.

TROUBLESHOOTING

Unfortunately, we live in a world where nothing operates at peak performance forever. All good things must pass, and all things will eventually fail. The desire is to keep them from failing for as long as practical and then recover as quickly as possible. The following tips fall into the category of trying to keep the entire system running and recovering when it doesn't.

Check that compression is active. If the local drive is supposed to be compressed, yet it is not compressing, verify that DBLSPACE.SYS appears in the CONFIG.SYS file.

Check that drivers are loading. If the hard drive is compressed and drivers that should be loading are not, or the workstation is not connecting to the network, then verify that DBLSPACE.SYS is in the CONFIG.SYS file on any other drivers, especially network drivers.

Check server drives. If the workstation connects to the network but cannot see the first server drive, F:, the problem can be due to DBLSPACE acting as though it is using that drive for its operations.

Instead of using MAP F:= in the login script, use MAP *1:= and add the following two lines in DBLSPACE.INI:

```
FirstDrive=E
LastDrive=E
```

Usually, if you have the network running before starting the utility to compress the local drive, DBLSPACE will see that F: is a network drive, and this problem will not occur.

Verify that COMMAND.COM can be found. If you're constantly getting messages that COMMAND.COM cannot be loaded after you've been using the workstation for a while, check the login script to see if it is setting the COMSPEC variable. If so, edit the

SHELL command line in CONFIG.SYS and make certain that the path to COMMAND.COM points to the root directory and not to a subdirectory.

Look for hanging screen savers. If a screen blanker is active on a workstation, and you cannot get it to go off no matter what keys you press, try pressing the Ctrl-Enter keys. If someone sent a message to the workstation, the message is waiting to be cleared by this key combination before returning processing to the keyboard.

To keep others from sending you messages, use CASTOFF from the SEND command.

Changing the node address on a network board can create conflicts with other boards in the workstation. Use the hard-coded node address whenever possible.

Use common sense when you're setting up workstations, and treat them as if they are servers. By that, I mean to keep all components grounded and to label cables. Keep the machines clean and serviced on a regular basis. Pay attention to the ambient environment, and try to keep it as clean as possible.

Chapter 10, "Troubleshooting," discusses error messages, but the majority of them pertain to the NetWare operating system and not to DOS. Following is a list of the more common error messages on a workstation:

- *Abort, retry, fail?*—This message is the standard error any time a call is made to a device that cannot be found. Verify that you typed the command properly. If so, then try again. If that does not work, then reboot and try again.

- *Access denied*—Either the username or the password was entered incorrectly. Have the user try again. If intruder detection is turned on, the user can try only a certain number of times before he or she is locked out. As a system administrator, you must re-enable the login before the user will be able to get in.

- *A File Server could not be found*—The shell tried to connect to a network but could not find it. From another workstation, verify that the server is indeed up and then try again. If it still fails, check the NIC card.

- *Bad or missing filename*—The CONFIG.SYS file made a call to a nonexistent file. Check CONFIG.SYS and verify the existence of the file in the path given.

- *Cannot RECOVER a Network drive*—You cannot recover files from a drive on the server with DOS. Use SALVAGE if you are trying to restore a deleted file.

- *Convert lost chains to files?*—CHKDSK has found errors in the File Allocation Table. Running CHKDSK writes the errors to a file and resets the FAT to valid entries only. Files created take the format of FILExxxx.CHK and can be located easily in the root directory of the local hard drive.

- *EXEC failure*—This message can indicate a corrupted executable, but most often the "Files=" statement in CONFIG.SYS is set too low. Increase the number, reboot the workstation and try again.

- *File creation error*—DOS will not allow you to create a file with the name of a file that already exists. Try again with a different name.

- *Internal stack overflow*—DOS was trying to use more stacks than were available. Reboot.

- *Invalid COMMAND.COM*—Part of the DOS memory area has been overwritten by an application, and now the operating system cannot find the COMSPEC variable that it needs. The only solution is to reboot.

- *Memory allocation error*—Reboot. If the problem persists, then reinstall the operating system files.

- *Message not sent to ....*—Whoever you are trying to send the message to is using CASTOFF, or the buffer that exists for incoming messages on that workstation is full. The solution?

Go back to work and stop heckling Bill for installing his applications in the root directory.

- *Network Error during .... Abort, Retry or Fail?*—Either a DOS function call could not be performed, or the server is down. Verify that the server is up; then try the call once more.

- *No free file handles*—You cannot restart COMMAND.COM after an operation. Reboot. If the problem persists, then increase the number of files in the CONFIG.SYS file.

- *Seek error...*—The information requested cannot be found. Verify that the request is valid.

MOVING ON

In this chapter, you learned about workstations—one of the most crucial components of a network. They can run different operating systems. Additionally, you can optimize and troubleshoot them with the information you learned here.

In the next chapter, "Windows Marvels," we'll look at a growing component of workstations everywhere and the way Windows interacts with NetWare.

Chapter 8
WINDOWS MARVELS

The computing world is gravitating more toward graphical interfaces with every passing day, and the continent of networking is no exception. Users want their workstation operations to be as simplified and "user-friendly" as possible. Condensing a wordy string command to an icon mimics effortless operations, even if it is only perceived by the users to be that way.

At home, Bob can double-click a mouse on a picture of a checkerboard, and suddenly he's playing chess against his favorite cartoon opponents. If that is the case at home, then Bob asks, why can't I, at work, double-click the mouse and access the file server?

The answer is that Bob can.

There are several parameters that must be set, and there are a few problem areas where things may not work under all conditions, but these areas can be attributed to the fact that the marriage of Windows and NetWare is still in the honeymoon stage. The sections that follow in this chapter will discuss all aspects of Windows as they relate to operations from a workstation into the NetWare operating system.

SETTING UP

Before you can use Windows to access the server, you must first install it on the workstation. The following tips relate to that installation. The last section of this chapter covers troubleshooting, in case you already have Windows installed, and all is not working as it should.

 The minimum requirements for a workstation to run Windows are as follows:

- *80286 processor or higher.* In my opinion, you should consider a 386 the minimum and give a 486 serious consideration. Although Windows will run on a 286, it will do so only in standard mode and not enhanced. It will be SL-O-O-OW.

- *1mb of extended memory on a 286, and 2mb on a 386 or higher.* Give serious thought to having 4mb of extended memory.

- *5mb to 11mb hard drive space.* This amount depends on how many options you include in the installation.

- *DOS 3.1 or higher.* Earnestly think 5.0 or higher to maximize your efficiency.

 Installation is straightforward. To install Windows on the workstation, insert the disks in the floppy drive and run the Install-Setup program. The only real choice you're given is a selection for a Custom or Express setup; under most circumstances, the Express setup is sufficient. Do verify, however, that it recognizes the network before you continue on past that screen.

 To enable Windows and NetWare on a workstation, perform the following steps:

1. From inside the workstation's Windows, choose Run from the File menu, and put the NetWare Windows Workstation Services disk in the floppy drive.

2. At the command line, enter the floppy designation and NWSETUP. For example, type **A:\NWSETUP**.

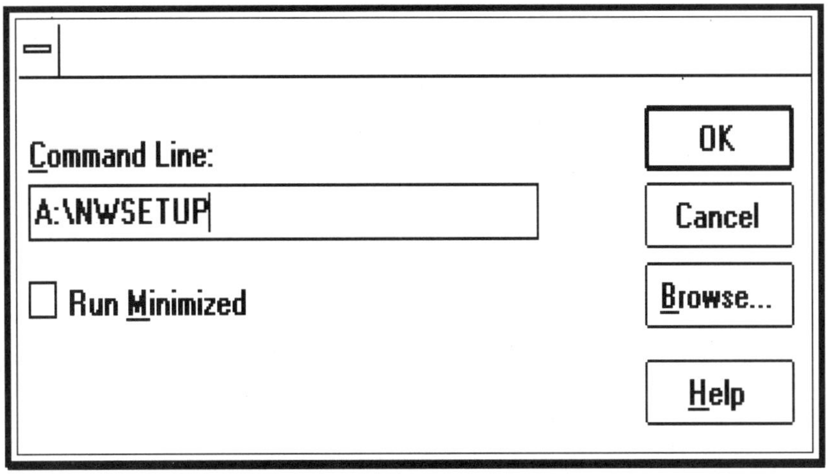

```
 ┌──────────────────────────────────────────────────────────┐
 │ ┌───┐                                                      │
 │ │ ─ │                                                      │
 │ └───┘                                                      │
 │                                                            │
 │                                            ┌────────────┐  │
 │   Command Line:                            │     OK     │  │
 │  ┌──────────────────────────────────────┐ └────────────┘  │
 │  │ A:\NWSETUP│                           │ ┌────────────┐  │
 │  └──────────────────────────────────────┘ │   Cancel   │  │
 │                                            └────────────┘  │
 │   ☐ Run Minimized                          ┌────────────┐  │
 │                                            │  Browse... │  │
 │                                            └────────────┘  │
 │                                            ┌────────────┐  │
 │                                            │    Help    │  │
 │                                            └────────────┘  │
 └──────────────────────────────────────────────────────────┘
```

Figure 8-1: Setting up a NetWare workstation to run with Windows requires the Windows installation procedure.

3. Follow the instructions that appear on the screen and then reboot the workstation.

4. Log into the workstation, on bootup, as ADMIN, and move to the PUBLIC subdirectory.

5. From that subdirectory, copy a file named NWADMIN.INI to the local hard drive, in the WINDOWS subdirectory.

6. Start Windows, and using the Program Manager File menu, choose New and then Program Item. After you enter a description in the designated field, type the path of the NWADMIN.EXE file into the Command Line field (this path should be the same as the PUBLIC subdirectory; thus, if the Public subdirectory in step 4 was Z, then you'd type **Z:\NWADMIN.EXE**).

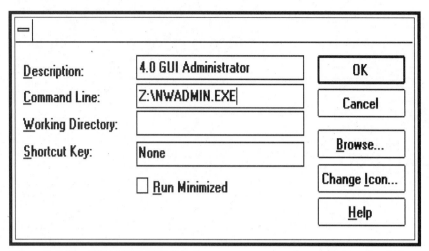

Figure 8-2: The NWADMIN.EXE file gives you access to the administrative GUI utility in NetWare 4.0.

 The following files come with Windows and are used in the networking setup:

- *NETWARE.DRV.* The device driver.

- *NETWARE.INI.* The initialization file for the driver. If it does not exist, it gets created.

- *NETWARE.HLP.* The help file.

- *NWPOPUP.EXE.* The processor used for broadcast messages that come into the workstation.

- *VNETWARE.386.* Virtual NetWare device driver for 386 Enhanced mode.

- *VIPX.386.* Virtual IPX driver for 386 Enhanced mode.

You can think of NETWARE.DRV as the go-between for Windows applications and the network through the NIC card and the files NETX, IPXODI, LSL and MLID.

The purpose of NETX. When a message comes in to the workstation, NETX is the file responsible for notifying Windows of the message. VNETWARE.386 coordinates the message

reception and calls the NWPOPUP file, which then displays the
message dialog.

 **Parameters that Windows uses to know that it is supposed to
communicate with a network are contained in the SYSTEM.INI
file.** Within this file, the relevant entries and subheadings (enclosed
in brackets [ ]) are as follows:

```
[boot]
network.drv=netware.drv
[boot.description]
network.drv=Novell NetWare
[386Enh]
network=*vnetbios,vnetware.386,vipx.386
PagingFile=C:\WINDOWS\WIN386.SWP
MaxPagingFileSize=1024
```

VNETBIOS is the virtual network BIOS, and PagingFile is where
temporary swap files will be generated and stored. Remember to
always make PagingFile local. Diskless workstations must have different swap file names, otherwise, they will become corrupted if they're
trying to operate in the same directory as other workstations.
MaxPagingFileSize gives the size of each file that will be swapped in
and out. The absolute minimum is 1mb, and 4mb, or 4096, is highly
recommended.

Temporary directories must be created. The Windows software requires temporary directories where it can store files that
are open and other items it needs for each operation. Never should
that temporary directory reside on the server. If it does, the amount
of network traffic is increased, and access time is decreased. Not only
does the workstation running Windows run slower as information is
transferred back and forth, but all other workstations suffer from the
increased workload on the server and traffic on the line. The temporary directories should reside on local drives whenever possible.

With diskless workstations, having temporary directories, of course,
is not possible, and they should be considered poor choices for Windowed workstations.

Consider loading Windows on the server. You can install Windows on the server, letting several workstations access it, and still have the temporary drives residing on the local drive of each workstation. For Windows 3.0, leave 11mb of server space, and leave an additional 5mb—for a total of 16mb—if you're using version 3.1.

DR DOS files need to be dated 4/7/92 or later in order to run Windows without hanging. Additionally, the CONFIG.SYS file on each workstation must install the EMM386.SYS driver on every power-up.

Add more mb for the graphical interface. If a workstation is going to run the NetWare Administrator graphical interface, it needs Windows 3.0 or 3.1, an 80386 or higher processor and approximately 8mb RAM, although you can squeeze by with 6mb.

A minimum of 60 open files is required at the workstation. I strongly encourage 80. Verify this number by looking in the CONFIG.SYS and NET.CFG files for the following line:

```
FILE HANDLES=60
```

Be careful of the COMSPEC variable, which tells applications where to find the DOS command interpreter. Some applications will overwrite the area where DOS is storing this information, and you will get an "Invalid COMMAND.COM" message. If you get this message, the only solution to get running again is to reboot the workstation.

TASK SWITCHING

Task switching is the act of leaving one application, without exiting from it, and going to another application. The one that was exited may continue processing, if a request was made of it, or may wait patiently for the user to come back to it.

Much discussion with Windows revolves around whether it is running in standard or enhanced mode. Standard mode, quite simply, means that a workstation can have several windows open at one time, but only one is processing; all others stop processing when that window is not active.

With enhanced mode, applications can continue to run in the background while the user is working in another window. For example, a floppy disk can be formatted in the drive while the user is busy putting finishing touches on a spreadsheet.

NetWare's task switching allows non-Windows programs to work in the multitasking environment. You must use it if you will be switching between DOS sessions and running in standard or real mode. You do not need it if you're running in enhanced mode or not switching between DOS sessions. If you're unsure about whether you need task switching or not, install it as follows:

1. Expand the files TBM12.COM and TASKID.COM from the NetWare disk by typing:

   ```
   Unpack A:TBM12.CO_ C:TMB12.COM
   Unpack A:TASKID.CO_ C:TASKID.COM
   ```

2. Type **TBM12**.

3. Start Windows.

4. Start a DOS session.

5. At a prompt, type **TASKID**.

For each DOS session you open, run TASKID within the window before running any applications from the command line. When you close a DOS session with the Exit command, unload TASKID by typing **TASKID /U**.

Always unload TASKID. If you don't unload TASKID in a session before closing it, the workstation may have a tendency to hang and need to be rebooted.

TASKID command-line parameters are as follows:

/? or /H	Help.
/C{filename}	Use a file other than NET.CFG for configuration information.
/D	Display diagnostic information.
/I	Display version information.
/U	Unload from memory.

COMCHECK and RCONSOLE require too many buffers to use with TMB12. You must unload TBM12 with the "/U" option before you can use either of them.

INCREASING PERFORMANCE

The following tips will help you interact with the Windows and NetWare systems more efficiently.

You can have Windows start without displaying the welcome screen by specifying the following at the command line:

```
WIN :
```

Or you can have it immediately start the program you want to be working on if you follow WIN with the name of the program to run. For example,

```
WIN SOL
```

Note: You must, however, be in the directory where the program you are attempting to start resides or you will get a "Directory could not be found" error message.

This command starts Windows and immediately begins the Solitaire program.

Start Windows immediately after the login. You can add F: and EXIT "WIN" to login scripts so that when the login is created, Windows is automatically started up.

Two of the most important features of Windows are the Program Manager and the File Manager. You use Program Manager to create and coordinate Windows icons, applications and so on. You use File Manager, on the other hand, to copy, rename, move and delete files, etc. You should learn the interworkings of these two features to become Windows literate.

Never run CHKDSK /f in a Windows session. The "/F" option looks for open files and assumes them to be errors in the File Allocation Table. It closes the files—which can be files Windows needed to operate or other Windows sessions running in the background—and changes the FAT.

NetWare provides Windows dialog boxes that allow you to set up your network environment. Using the NWADMIN utility, you are able to initialize and change all variables, including the following:

- Device Setup

- Manage Drive Mappings

- Manage Printing

- Manage Network Connections

- Send Messages

- Set a Hotkey

A *hotkey* is a function key that provides a single point of access to network dialog boxes. The default is the F6 key.

Under Manage Printing, you can define the number of print jobs that can be stored in the print manager queue. The default is 50, with a maximum of 250 and a minimum of 1.

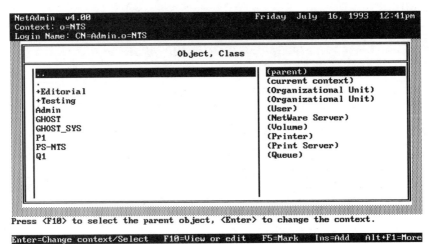

```
NetAdmin  v4.00                        Friday  July  16, 1993  12:41pm
Context: o=NTS
Login Name: CN=Admin.o=NTS

                          Object, Class

 ..                                  (parent)
 .                                   (current context)
 +Editorial                          (Organizational Unit)
 +Testing                            (Organizational Unit)
 Admin                               (User)
 GHOST                               (NetWare Server)
 GHOST_SYS                           (Volume)
 P1                                  (Printer)
 PS-NTS                              (Print Server)
 Q1                                  (Queue)




Press <F10> to select the parent object, <Enter> to change the context.

Enter=Change context/Select   F10=View or edit   F5=Mark   Ins=Add   Alt+F1=More
```

Figure 8-3: The NetWare Administrator lets you view and manage information about the objects on your NetWare 4.0 network.

 The NetWare Administrator is set up so that you can view or edit information about an object in one place—the object dialog. NetWare print services have three different objects: servers, printers and queues. Each has its own object dialog.

 To start up the NetWare Administrator graphical interface and add or modify the printing setup, follow these steps:

1. Log into a Directory Services server.

2. Copy the NWADMIN.INI from SYS:PUBLIC to the Windows directory where other INI files are.

3. Start Windows from a workstation.

4. Select the group from which you want to start the NetWare Administrator.

5. From the Program Manager File menu, choose the New option.

6. Select the Program Item button and choose OK.

7. Type **NetWare Administrator** in the description field.

8. Type **NWADMIN.EXE** in the Command Line field, and choose OK.

To exit the NetWare Administrator, go to the Object menu and choose Exit, press Alt-F4 or double-click the System menu box.

 Keep the Browser window open. If you accidentally close the Browser window, you can reopen it by going to the Tools menu and choosing Browser.

 To open a printing object dialog to make changes relative to printing operations, follow these steps:

1. Double-click leaf objects in the directory tree or single-click on container objects in the directory tree.

2. Choose Details from the Object menu or right-click the mouse on any object in the directory tree.

3. Choose Details from the menu that appears, or when you're creating a new object in the Create dialog, choose the Define Additional Properties box and then choose Create.

Information in the object dialog is divided into "pages" you view one at a time. OK and Cancel affect the entire dialog, not just the page you're currently viewing. To save the changes to every page, choose OK; a confirmation box then allows you to verify your choice. To return to the Browser without changing any pages, click Cancel.

Because the pages are all part of one dialog box, do not choose OK or Cancel until you're finished with all pages and are ready to close the dialog box. OK assumes you are done and returns you to the Browser.

If you specify changes in several pages and decide you don't want to keep some of the changes, you need to delete the unwanted information manually from the fields.

Consider minimizing icon directories to only those you use the most. Minimizing directories keeps the screen from being cluttered with icons you may rarely use. Microsoft recommends that no more than 40 icons be used on a menu.

Reduce the space icons occupy. If you do have many icons, the descriptions beneath them usually take up more room than the icons themselves and can become garbled with the descriptions of icons surrounding them.

For icons with obvious meanings, you can remove the descriptions by choosing Program Item Properties from the Program Manager and pressing the spacebar at the Description field. Doing this leaves the icon and removes the text description. Click OK, and you're finished.

Modify workstations with parallel printers. If you want network users to access a parallel printer cabled to a workstation running Windows 3.0, add the following lines to the SYSTEM.INI file before loading NPRINTER.EXE:

```
LPR1AutoAssign=0
LPT1irq=-1
```

To do the same thing with a serial printer and avoid conflicts with COM ports, make the following entries:

```
COM1AutoAssign=0
COM1irq=-1
```

Use the Alt-Tab combination to toggle between the two most recently used programs. This moves you back and forth between the two screens most recently accessed.

You can skip the mouse altogether and jump to keyboard choices by pressing the Alt key. This will cause the menus to appear from the top of the screen.

TROUBLESHOOTING

The tips that follow will hopefully help you iron out some of the difficulties present in trying to get an interface as complicated as Windows to talk to an operating system as different from it as Net-Ware. As with most troubleshooting, the greatest tool of all in solving the problem is common sense. Try to isolate the problem to its lowest denominator by listing possibilities and experimenting. Only when you know what one item is causing the problem can you begin to correct it.

If you're loading TSRs or third-party applications directly from the CONFIG.SYS file, one of your first steps should always be to unload these applications and try again. They could be causing conflicts, and isolating them is a very simple process that you can do in a matter of minutes. If the problem still exists, then you at least know that they are not causing the problem, and you can proceed from there.

Conflicts can occur with addresses. If NWSETUP hangs when you're trying to load Windows, the problem is probably due to the fact that Windows uses the I/O address 2E0H. If the network board inside the workstation is also using this address, it is causing conflict, and you must change the board address.

If you cannot connect to a network drive, make sure you have the correct network drivers. Choose Windows Setup application in the Main group and read the Network line from the four listed. It should say "Novell NetWare." If the setting is wrong, choose the Options-Change System Settings command, and choose a different driver from the network list.

Check upper memory. If you have problems running Windows while the network driver is in upper memory, try loading one or the other in conventional memory. An easy way to do this is to start Windows with the following command:

```
WIN /D:X
```

The "X" parameter means to exclude the XMS memory for Windows. If all works—as it should now—the shared RAM area used by the NIC is not excluded from the memory manager or the Windows internal memory manager.

When you lose connection to the network, Windows 3.0 will give you an error box with choices of Cancel or Retry. These choices do not correspond to the DOS choices—Abort, Retry or Cancel—and choosing one of the Windows choices will hang the system. You must reboot to go back to work.

Don't overlook the advantage of SMARTDRV.EXE. If you plan to run Windows on each workstation's hard disk and access local files extensively, then install SMARTDRV.EXE in the AUTOEXEC.BAT of each workstation. Otherwise, don't run SMARTDRV.EXE at all because it is a caching utility, and NetWare already provides caching.

When you're in File Manager, often you can't back up from the subdirectory that is showing to the parent directory beneath. You can't back up because the two dots (..) representing the parent directory are not represented and cannot be clicked. To change this situation, add the following line to the NET.CFG file:

```
SHOW DOTS=ON
```

Keep drive mapping changes. By default, drive mappings made inside a window are good only for that window and not for other windows that are currently open or ones you later open. If you want drive mappings to be saved when you exit, set the Restore-Drives switch in SYSTEM.INI to False, as follows:

```
[NetWare]
RestoreDrives=false
```

Use NWShareHandles=true, under the same heading, to enable the new drive mappings to be shared globally among all windows presently open.

Changing one window then changes all windows. If NWShare-Handles is set to True, however, then changing a directory on a network drive in one window can affect all other windows you have open. Whether or not to use this parameter is up to a user's discretion. There are six points in favor of using it, and half a dozen against.

In the absence of network printing, windowed applications send their print jobs to the Print Manager. The Print Manager then spools the jobs out to the attached printer.

With network printing, the job is still sent to the Print Manager, which spools the job and then sends the job out to the intended port. This job is intercepted by the NetWare shell, which sends the job to the print queue for spooling. After spooling is done, the print server receives the job and begins printing it. In other words, the job is spooled twice, and the printing time is greatly increased.

Print Manager's purpose is to spool a print job and send it to the printer, whereas NetWare spools jobs waiting for the timeout after each end-of-job. Having the two running together is wasteful. To increase print performance, you must first disable the Print Manager:

1. Open the control panel from the Main group in Program Manager.

2. Open the Printers program.

3. Clear the "Use Print Manager" check box, and click Close to save the settings.

To delete an application, highlight its icon and press Del. However, this process still leaves descriptions regarding the application in WIN.INI—the file that is read before every startup. It slows down the time it takes for the Windows software to load.

To correct this problem, edit WIN.INI and remove all lines referring to the deleted program. The program's name will be in brackets, and all lines referring to it will be beneath and go down to the next program name. Following is a portion of a sample WIN.INI file, with all references to the America Online program highlighted:

```
[windows]
spooler=yes
load=nwpopup.exe,C:\REACHOUT\reachout.exe
run=
Beep=No
NullPort=None
BorderWidth=1
CursorBlinkRate=827
DoubleClickSpeed=343
Programs=com exe bat pif
Documents=
DeviceNotSelectedTimeout=15
TransmissionRetryTimeout=45
KeyboardDelay=2
KeyboardSpeed=31
ScreenSaveActive=1
ScreenSaveTimeOut=120
device=Generic / Text Only,TTY,LPT1:
MouseTrails=-7
MouseThreshold1=4
MouseThreshold2=12
MouseSpeed=2
CoolSwitch=1

[WAOL]
WPFLAGS=2
WPSHOWCMD=3
WPPTMINPOSX=0
WPPTMINPOSY=0
WPPTMAXPOSX=0
WPPTMAXPOSY=0
WPNPOSTOP=0
WPNPOSBOT=480
WPNPOSLEFT=0
WPNPOSRIGHT=640

[sounds]
SystemAsterisk=chord.wav,Asterisk
SystemHand=chord.wav,Critical Stop
SystemDefault=ding.wav,Default Beep
SystemExclamation=chord.wav,Exclamation
SystemQuestion=chord.wav,Question
SystemExit=chimes.wav,Windows Exit
SystemStart=tada.wav,Windows Start
Welcome=Welcome.wav
```

```
Goodbye=Goodbye.wav
IM=IM.wav
File's Done=FileDone.wav
You've Got Mail=GotMail.wav
```

The entire highlighted section would be removed to prevent Windows from continuing to refer to it.

If a workstation does not receive broadcast messages while in Windows... Make certain NWPOPUP.EXE is included in the WIN.INI file. If it is listed there, check the control panel and go into Network Options to verify that the Messages Enabled check box is marked with an "X."

If a workstation locks up... If broadcast messages appear on the workstation but lock up the Windows program, check for a GET LOCAL TARGET STACKS line in the NET.CFG file. If this line is not present, then add it.

If Windows takes a long time to load on a workstation, there are several possibilities as to why. The first order of business is to clean up the WIN.INI file by deleting program lines for which you've deleted the program icons. The second is to verify where the temporary swap file is loading to and make sure that it is to a local drive and not across the network.

If garbage prints on the network printer when you attempt to print from Windows... Increase the amount of timeout (TI) in the CAPTURE statement before loading Windows. Another print job could be coming behind the current job and corrupting it.

If the workstation is going to print exclusively from Windows, I recommend you use the following line:

```
CAPTURE TI=0
```

This line cancels the timeout feature and causes the whole job to be received before printing starts.

Watch for duplicate print jobs. If the printer prints more than one copy of the print job, look under the Link Driver section in the NET.CFG file. You should see a line saying "Double Buffer." If it isn't there, then add it.

If Windows hangs when you're opening a DOS window... Check the interrupt levels, and see if there are any other problems besides this one. For example, does Windows hang at any other point or only when you're trying to open a DOS window? If it hangs only when you're opening a DOS window, you've reduced the likelihood of an interrupt problem, and the solution should be to increase the number of File Handles (60 is required, and 80 is recommended).

MOVING ON

This chapter discussed only one item—the working relationship between Microsoft Windows on workstations and Novell's NetWare operating system on the network. The two can work together if all variables are properly defined in the Windows initialization files (SYSTEM.INI and WIN.INI) and there are no conflicts between interrupts used by Windows and those used by anything else.

The next chapter, "Miscellaneous Alchemy," is an accumulation of stray tips that allow NetWare 4.0 to function better, with particular emphasis on auditing and server utilities.

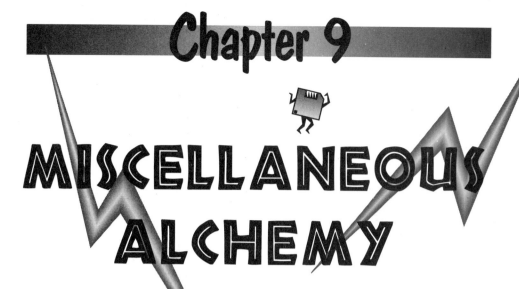

Chapter 9

MISCELLANEOUS ALCHEMY

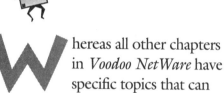

Whereas all other chapters in *Voodoo NetWare* have specific topics that can contain several subtopics, this chapter is an anomaly. Its purpose is to cover topics that do not conveniently fall into any other category.

We start by covering the concept of trustees and then move into the functions of auditing. From there, we take a sharp left and drive through server utilities, only to end up by discussing true miscellany that can be broken down no further.

TRUSTEES

A *trustee* is a user or, more often, a group of users who have been given rights to work with directories and files. You must assign the rights individually to each directory and/or file the trustee will be able to access, and these rights filter downward. For example, if you make a user a trustee of a file, he or she has the granted rights to that file only. If you gave the rights to a directory, however, then the user has those rights for every file in the directory.

As stated, you can grant trustee rights to individual users or to groups. When they're assigned to groups, the rights are effective for every member of the group. For this reason, trustee rights are a key component of system security and should not be looked upon lightly.

 NetWare 4.0 offers the following nine different types of rights that you can assign to trustees:

Supervisory	All rights.
None	No rights.
Read	Read from files.
Write	Write to and modify files.
Create	Make new files and subdirectories.
Erase	Delete existing files and subdirectories.
Modify	Change existing subdirectories and files.
File Scan	See file and subdirectory names in the file system structure.
Access Control	Add and change rights to files and subdirectories.

 The danger in having trustee rights begins when users are assigned Access Control\Supervisory rights. They can then change rights for themselves and other users.

Be particularly careful when you add a user to a group, or use one user's template as the basis for another, that you are not giving away permissions that you would rather not.

AUDITING

Auditing is a method of examining records to be certain that network transactions are accurate. You can audit Directory Services events as well as those specific to a volume, file system or server. With NetWare version 4.0, auditing programs are automatically installed with the software. These programs let you keep a record of the following:

- *File directory events.* Tells when they are created, modified, deleted and so on.

- *Server events.* Tells when the server is downed, mounted, dismounted, and when a modification is done to security.

- *Directory Services events.* Tells when objects are added, moved, renamed or deleted.

Auditing is easily enabled. To enable auditing of a volume, type **AUDITCON** at the command prompt at a DOS workstation and choose Enable Volume Auditing from the Available Audit Options menu. Enter a password for the volume and reenter it again at the prompt.

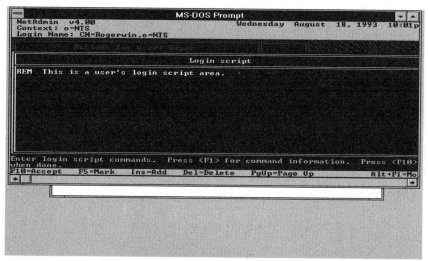

Figure 9-1: With the AUDITCON utility, a NetWare 4.0 administrator can audit volumes on network file servers.

Auditing of Directory Services can be activated. To enable auditing of Directory Services, type **AUDITCON** at the command prompt at a DOS workstation and choose Audit Directory Services from the Available Audit Options menu. Select Audit Directory Tree from a container and press F10. Enter a password for the container and reenter it again at the prompt.

AUDITCON serves many purposes. Use AUDITCON to change the password, create audit reports and do all the functions that were available in previous versions with ATOTAL and PAUDIT.

Server monitoring software packages are available. They can check traffic counting, do protocol analyzing, network inventory and extended network management and control. You can also have them report and notify you of alarm conditions. A good example is LANAlert from Network Computing, Inc., in San Jose.

For notification, some monitoring packages can dial a pager or fax number to notify the administrator of an emergency condition. Almost all of them do reporting and statistical analysis, as well as hard disk monitoring.

Large installations should consider inventory applications. LAN inventory software that automatically compiles a list of the hardware and software components of the workstations on a network is available. This software saves the administrator a good bit of footwork by letting him or her know immediately what is on the network and what is available.

Some of these programs work in the foreground and do their compiling on each login of the workstation. Compiling at this time slows the login process down slightly but is usually nothing too noticeable. Other programs are TSRs that work in the background. Although they do not slow logins down any, they consume RAM that could be better allocated elsewhere.

SERVER UTILITIES

Many utilities included with NetWare can be run only from the console and are of importance only to the system administrator. These utilities consist of console commands and loadable modules, or "NLMs," as they are often called.

If they are commands, you can enter them directly at the server console prompt. If they are loadable modules, then you must load them into memory using the LOAD process. An alphabetic listing of both types of utilities follows.

ABORT REMIRROR

This command stops the remirroring of a logical partition.

 Use ABORT REMIRROR when you have to swap a drive and cannot afford to bring the server down. After you're finished, start remirroring again with REMIRROR PARTITION.

ADD NAME SPACE

This utility lets you store non-DOS files (MAC, UNIX) on a NetWare volume. The correct syntax is as follows:

```
ADD NAME SPACE name [TO [VOLUME]] volume_name.
```

You need to execute it only once for each non-DOS naming convention it is to store.

 This utility cannot be immediately run. ADD NAME SPACE is a loadable module; you must load the name space module LOAD before you can use it.

BIND

BIND links LAN drivers to a communication protocol and to a specific network board in the server. Unless you link a communication protocol to the board, it cannot process packets.

You may not need to use BIND because it is added after the LAN driver in AUTOEXEC.NCF as an IPX. If you're using other protocols, then you will not need this utility.

BROADCAST

This utility sends messages to one or all users. There is a 55-character maximum on the message sent.

 BROADCAST can be used with multiple users. When you're using BROADCAST, separate the names of multiple users with a comma (,) or a space or the word "and."

Be certain the user you are sending to is present. The receiving user's workstation will not process anything else until the screen message is cleared.

 To send a message to a specific user, specify the user's entire object structure. For example, the following line sends the message throughout the network, across the servers and directly to Karen Scott in the training department of ARC:

```
BROADCAST "Need a ride home" To
CN=kscott.OU=training.O=ARC
```

To send a message to two users, follow the same idea, but specify both users' object structures:

```
Broadcast "Meeting @ 6" To
CN=kscott.OU=training.O=ARC,CN=ljames.OU=drivers.O=N_AMERICAN
```

This line sends the message to Karen Scott and Landon James.

CDROM

CDROM allows the server to use a CD-ROM disk as a Read-only volume. The syntax is as follows:

```
LOAD [path] CDROM
```

If no path is specified, the server looks for CDROM in SYS:SYSTEM.

CLEAR STATION n

The CLEAR STATION n utility cancels the connection between the server and workstation, where *n* is the number obtained from the Monitor screen.

 Clear the station only when data will not be damaged. If the workstation is in the middle of a transaction when you use CLEAR STATION n, the file may be saved with incorrect or unchanged data.

CLIB

CLIB is a library of routines and functions.

CLS

You use CLS to clear the server console screen.

You can use OFF to do the same thing as the CLS command. Both fulfill the same function.

CONFIG

The CONFIG utility displays the NetWare server name, the internal network number of the server, loaded LAN drivers, hardware settings on all network boards, the node address of the network boards, the communication protocol bound to the network board, the network number of the cabling scheme for a network board, the frame type assigned to a board and the board name assigned.

DISABLE LOGIN

This command is self-explanatory; it's the toggle of ENABLE LOGIN.

DISABLE TTS

Use DISABLE TTS to free up server memory and test transactional applications with it disabled. The antithesis of this command is ENABLE TTS.

DISKSET

The DISKSET utility places the ID about external hard disks on an EPROM chip of the host bus adapter, formats external hard disks and backs up NetWare Ready configuration information from a NetWare Ready disk to another disk. The syntax is as follows:

```
LOAD [path] DISKSET
```

DISMOUNT volume_name

You use DISMOUNT volume_name to make a volume unavailable to users.

DISPLAY NETWORKS

This utility lists all networks and assigned numbers that a server router recognizes.

DISPLAY SERVERS

The DISPLAY SERVERS utility lists all recognized servers.

DOMAIN

Use DOMAIN to create a protected operating system domain to test and develop NLMs in rings 1, 2 or 3. After they're checked out, then they can run in the live ring 0.

DOWN

You use DOWN to ensure data integrity by writing all cache buffers to disk, closing all files and updating appropriate Directory and File Allocation Tables.

 After the server is downed, it continues to receive packets. You can track them by using TRACK ON and TRACK OFF.

DSREPAIR

DSREPAIR repairs and corrects problems in the Directory Services database. The syntax is as follows:

```
LOAD [path] DSREPAIR
```

Directory files are locked during the DSREPAIR operation. You must exit completely to unlock.

EDIT

Use EDIT to create or modify a text file. The syntax is as follows:

```
LOAD [path] EDIT
```

ENABLE LOGIN

This command is the opposite of DISABLE LOGIN.

ENABLE TTS

You use ENABLE TTS to start transaction tracking.

EXIT

Using EXIT, you return to DOS after downing the file server.

INSTALL

With INSTALL, your choices are almost endless. You can create, delete or modify disk partitions; install Directory Services; load and unload disk and LAN drivers; mirror or unmirror hard drives; create, delete, expand, modify, mount or dismount volumes; create and format a DOS partition; create or modify AUTOEXEC.NCF and STARTUP.NCF; copy NetWare files onto the server; execute a surface test for bad blocks; install and configure products on server; add licensing information to the license disk; or add registration information to the registration disk. The syntax is as follows:

```
LOAD [path] INSTALL
```

 You can use INSTALL to copy the CD-ROM manuals onto the server, allowing all users to see. If you don't want everyone to see them, then set the permissions on the files as such.

IPXS

IPXS uses an NLM that requires STREAMS-based IPX protocol service. The syntax is as follows:

```
LOAD [path] IPXS
```

KEYB [parameter]

Use KEYB [parameter] to change the keyboard type for the server console. Parameters can be German, French, English, Spanish or Italian.

LANGUAGE

LANGUAGE sets the NLMs to use specific message files.

 LANGUAGE LIST will show you the available parameters, whereas LANGUAGE 7 or LANGUAGE GERMAN will change to German.

Other possibilities are as follows:

0	Canadian French
1	Chinese
2	Danish
3	Dutch
4	English
5	Finnish
6	French
7	German
8	Italian
9	Japanese
10	Korean
11	Norwegian
12	Portuguese
13	Russian
14	Spanish
15	Swedish

LIST DEVICES

The LIST DEVICES utility shows device information on the server.

LOAD

You use LOAD to load the NLMs.

MAGAZINE

This utility confirms magazine requests (insert or remove) from the server that have not yet been satisfied.

MATHLIB

Use MATHLIB if the server has a math coprocessor chip; you must load STREAMS and CLIB first. The syntax is as follows:

```
LOAD MATHLIB
```

MATHLIBC

Use MATHLIBC if the server does not have a math coprocessor; you still must load STREAMS and CLIB first.

MEDIA

MEDIA confirms media requests (insert and remove) from the server that have not yet been satisfied.

MEMORY

Use MEMORY to display the total amount of installed memory the operating system can address. On Micro Channel and ISA (AT bus) computers, NetWare can automatically address memory only up to 16mb, and you have to use REGISTER MEMORY to enable the operating system to address anything above this amount.

MIRROR STATUS

Use MIRROR STATUS to display all mirrored logical partitions and the status of each.

MODULES

MODULES displays the short name used to load each module and a descriptive string or long name for each module.

MONITOR

The MONITOR utility locks the server console and lets you view utilization and overall activity, as well as cached memory status, connections and their status, disk drives, mounted volumes, LAN drivers, loaded modules, file lock status and memory usage. The syntax is as follows:

```
LOAD [path] MONITOR
```

MOUNT volume_name or MOUNT ALL

You can use MOUNT volume_name or MOUNT ALL to make a volume accessible to users.

NAME

NAME shows the name of the server.

NMAGENT

Use NMAGENT to allow LAN drivers to register and pass network management parameters. The syntax is as follows:

```
LOAD [path] NMAGENT
```

NUT

NUT is short for **NLM User InTerface**. Use this utility if NLM requires this library of routines. Load it before the NLM requiring it.

NWSNUT

If an NLM requires this library of routines, load NWSNUT first.

OFF

Use OFF to clear the console screen.

PROTOCOL

Use PROTOCOL to view protocols registered on the server and register additional protocols. The syntax is as follows:

```
PROTOCOL or PROTOCOL REGISTER protocol frame id#
```

PSERVER

Use PSERVER to load the print server on the server. The syntax is as follows:

```
LOAD PSERVER printserver
```

 Before you can load the print server, you must use PCONSOLE to set up a print server and configuration file.

REGISTER MEMORY

REGISTER MEMORY allows NetWare to recognize RAM above 16mb. The syntax is as follows:

```
REGISTER MEMORY start_address length
```

Use the appropriate numbers in the following table for the variables *start* and *length*.

RAM	start	length
20mb	1000000	400000
24mb	1000000	800000
28mb	1000000	800000
32mb	1000000	1000000
36mb	1000000	1400000
40mb	1000000	1800000

To have the memory automatically loaded when the server is booted, add the REGISTER line to AUTOEXEC.NCF. This file is read each time the server is booted, and thus the additional memory will be automatically registered.

Be certain values are correctly entered. If the additional memory is not added when you use REGISTER MEMORY, check for an incorrect hexadecimal value for *start address* or *length*. If they appear correct, see if the *length* value is exceeding total installed memory.

REMIRROR PARTITION

REMIRROR PARTITION starts remirroring after an ABORT command.

REMOTE

Use REMOTE to allow remote access to the server console. The syntax is as follows:

```
LOAD [path] REMOTE [password]
```

 If you do not enter a password on the command line, NetWare will prompt you for one. This password is encrypted and is harder to see with a sniffer than if you enter it at the command line.

REMOVE DOS

Use REMOVE DOS to remove DOS from the server's memory and return the RAM for file caching. Removing the operating system increases security because loadable modules cannot be loaded from floppy drives. Also, this command enables the server to be warm booted when you use the EXIT command.

RESET ROUTER

Normally, a router updates its table every 2 minutes. With this utility, you can change the frequency with which a router updates its table.

ROUTE

The ROUTE command allows NetWare to send packets through bridges on a token ring cable. The syntax is as follows:

```
LOAD ROUTE
```

RPL

Use the RPL protocol to enable remote booting of IBM PC diskless workstations. The syntax is as follows:

```
LOAD REMOTE
LOAD RPL
```

RS232

The RS232 utility sets up a communications port for remote management. The syntax is as follows:

```
LOAD RS232 [ comm port ] [ modem speed ]
```

RSPX

You can use RSPX to allow the RCONSOLE utility to access a server. You must load REMOTE before RSPX as follows:

```
LOAD RSPX
```

RTDM

The RTDM utility enables data migration. The syntax is as follows:

```
LOAD RTDM
```

SCAN FOR NEW DEVICES

This utility checks disk hardware for changes since the last boot.

SEARCH

Use SEARCH to determine where to look for loadable module files and .NCF files; the default is SYS:SYSTEM. You can add other search paths or delete current ones and view the current paths. The syntax is as follows:

```
SEARCH or SEARCH [ADD [number] path]
SEARCH DEL number
```

 To check current search paths at the server console, type SEARCH without parameters. Other entries are as follows:

- SEARCH ADD A: adds a drive.

- SEARCH ADD 2 A: adds it as the second search path drive.

- SEARCH DEL 2 deletes the second path.

 SECURE CONSOLE disables SEARCH. You must bring the server down and reboot to create additional paths.

SECURE CONSOLE

The SECURE CONSOLE utility prevents loadable modules from loading (except modules from the SYS:SYSTEM) and prevents keyboard entry into the operating system debugger. It also prevents anyone other than the console operator from changing the date and time and removing DOS from the server.

SEND

Use SEND to send a message of 55 characters or less to a workstation user or users.

SERVER

Use SERVER to boot NetWare on the server, execute STARTUP.NCF, mount SYS and execute AUTOEXEC.NCF.

SERVMAN

You can use SERVMAN to view and configure operating system parameters; change .NCF files; change IPX/SPX configuration information; view adapter, device and disk partition information; view volume information; and view network information. The syntax is as follows:

```
LOAD SERVMAN
```

SET

Use SET to view operating system parameters and configure them to suit. These parameters include communications, memory, file caching, directory caching, file system, lock parameters, transaction tracking, disk parameters and time parameters. See Appendix B, "Setting Parameters," for a complete listing of parameters you can set.

One such parameter is SET TIME [month/day/year] or [hour:minute:second]. For example, enter the following line:

```
SET TIME 05/15/93 12:14:00
```

Another parameter is SET TIMEZONE, which configures information in CLIB used by modules. The default is Est5Edt.

SPEED

SPEED shows the speed at which the processor is running.

SPOOL

Use SPOOL to create, change or display spooler mappings.

SPXCONFIG

You can use SPXCONFIG to configure parameters of SPX. Use the syntax:

```
LOAD SPXCONFIG
```

SPXS

This utility provides STREAMS-based SPX protocol service. The syntax is as follows:

```
LOAD SPXS
```

STREAMS

With STREAMS, you can use loadable modules that require CLIB-loadable and STREAMS-based protocols. The syntax is as follows:

```
LOAD STREAMS
```

TIME

TIME shows the current server time.

TIMESYNC

With TIMESYNC, you can monitor internal time on the server to ensure that synchronization across the network is consistent. The syntax is as follows:

```
LOAD TIMESYNC
```

TLI

This utility provides TLI-communication services. The syntax is
as follows:

```
LOAD TLI
```

TRACK OFF

The TRACK OFF utility prevents the server from displaying packets
received or sent on the router tracking screen.

TRACK ON

This utility displays the router tracking screen as an active screen.

UNBIND

With UNBIND, you can remove a communication protocol from the
LAN driver of a network board or change the network number.

UNLOAD

Use UNLOAD to unload a loaded module.

 **If you plan to have the LAN driver unloaded for 15 minutes or
more, you should have users log out before unloading.** Under
15 minutes, they can still reconnect. Over that, they cannot.

UPS

Use the UPS utility to attach a UPS to the server. The syntax is
as follows:

```
LOAD UPS [type port discharge recharge]
```

For example, enter the following line:

```
LOAD UPS TYPE=DCB PORT=346 DISCHARGE=20 RECHARGE=120
```

 **Valid types of UPS are DCB, EDCB, STANDALONE, KEYCARD,
MOUSE, OTHER.** The default is DCB.

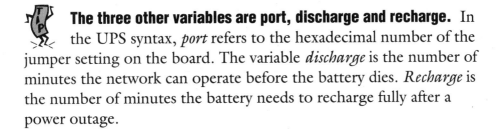 **The three other variables are port, discharge and recharge.** In the UPS syntax, *port* refers to the hexadecimal number of the jumper setting on the board. The variable *discharge* is the number of minutes the network can operate before the battery dies. *Recharge* is the number of minutes the battery needs to recharge fully after a power outage.

UPS STATUS

Use UPS STATUS to check the status of the uninterruptable power supply.

UPS TIME

With UPS TIME, you can change the discharge and recharge estimates. The syntax is as follows:

```
UPS TIME [DISCHARGE= RECHARGE=]
```

 Variables are not constantly updated. Changes you make with UPS TIME are not reflected on the screen until you run UPS STATUS again.

VERSION

Use VERSION to show the server version and copyright notice.

VOLUMES

With VOLUMES, you can list volumes mounted on the server.

VREPAIR

Use VREPAIR to correct volume problems and remove name space entries from the FAT and Directory Tables. The syntax is as follows:

```
LOAD VREPAIR
```

 VREPAIR will not run on a volume that is mounted. You must dismount the volume before repairs can be done.

Typically, if a volume is corrupted, you cannot mount it. Occasionally it will mount, but it causes an error in the process. Using VREPAIR can help if the problem was caused by a hardware failure or disk-read error. It can also be of assistance if a power failure has corrupted the volume or the console displays a mirroring error when the server boots.

MISCELLANY

The following tips are necessary, yet fall into no defined category.

In Chapter 6, "Printer Enchantment," you learned that serial printers use a DCE to DTE RS232-C protocol designed for connecting modems to PCs. One problem with modems, and likewise serial printers, is that many times you're trying to connect a 25-pin modem port to a 9-pin computer port. To solve this problem, you can buy an adapter at most computer stores or configure your own.

The following list, courtesy of William Steen at General Computing Services, Tipton, IN, shows the crossovers between a 25-pin and a 9-pin serial connection:

1	Data carrier [8]
2	Receive [3]
3	Transmit [2]
4	Data terminal ready [20]
5	Signal ground [7]
6	Data set ready [6]
7	Request to send [4]
8	Clear to send [5]
9	Ring indicator [22]

To begin mirroring and duplexing a drive, follow these steps:

1. Load Install.

2. Choose Maintenance/Selective Install from the Select An Installation Method menu.

3. Choose Disk Options from the Installation Options menu.

4. Choose Mirror/Unmirror Disk Partitions from the Available Disk Options.

5. Select a disk partition to mirror from the Disk Partition Mirroring Status list.

MOVING ON

All server utilities were discussed in alphabetic order in this chapter. You also learned about trustees and auditing. You should now have an understanding of the NetWare 4.0 operating system environment.

The next chapter, "Troubleshooting," discusses what to do when things that should work do not.

Chapter 10

TROUBLE-SHOOTING

f the world were a perfect place, the unemployment rate would jump to 50 percent. There would be no need for auto mechanics, VCR repairmen, plumbers, customer support or network troubleshooters. Thankfully for those gainfully employed in these professions, the world is not a perfect place. One of these days it may be, but when that day comes, we'll all be living on Sugar Candy Mountain and won't care much anyway.

This chapter contains a list of tips to consider when you're performing troubleshooting and follows that with an abbreviated listing of the most common error messages that are not discussed elsewhere. Chapter 6, "Printer Enchantment," contains errors relevant to printing problems. Other errors are covered in Chapters 7, "Workstation Wonders," and 8, "Windows Marvels," as they relate to workstations and Windows, respectively.

TIPS

The tips contained in this section will help you isolate problems to their source and correct them when possible.

Few objects are created at installation. When you first install the NetWare 4.0 operating system as a new install, the only objects that exist are the server, a SYS volume, an ADMIN user and any other volumes that you chose to create. Otherwise, all is bare.

When you upgrade from another version of NetWare, the existing objects become the ADMIN user, the server, and the previously existing volumes, users and groups.

For every directory tree created on installation, another ADMIN user is invented. This user has the rights to create other objects, and the supervisor must first log in as that user. After you've given Supervisor rights to other users, NetWare will allow you to rename ADMIN to something else.

Watch for stray characters. Illegal characters that you cannot use in the names of NetWare 4.0 objects include the question mark (?), asterisk (*), colon (:), comma (,), slash (/) and backslash (\).

An individual user can be a member of only one profile object. No more than one profile object can exist for a single user.

Check applications and avoid single-user packages. If an application does not run, make sure it is a multiuser network application and that search drives are mapped to the application.

Salvageable files are those saved by NetWare after they have been deleted. They are usually stored in the directory from which they were deleted. If a user deletes that directory, then they go into the DELETED.SAV subdirectory under the root directory.

Deleting files does not free disk space on the server, because the files are marked for removal but not actually removed. You must run PURGE for that to take effect. See Chapter 2, "Menu Magic," for information on PURGE and SALVAGE.

Under certain conditions, deleted files will be purged. If the server begins to run out of disk space, it will automatically start removing deleted files, beginning with the oldest deleted files.

 To check a server for suspected disk errors, go to the console and type the following at the console prompt:

```
LOAD Monitor
```

Choose Disk Information from the Available Options menu and then choose Disk Drive from the System Disk Drives menu. Write down the number of redirected blocks and compare the number with the last time you checked. If the number is increasing, troubleshoot the hard disk drive and controller.

To test for bad blocks on the server, follow these steps:

1. Make sure there is no activity on the server and then dismount each volume with the following command:

   ```
   DISMOUNT volume_name
   ```

2. Load INSTALL.

3. Choose Maintenance/Selective Install from Select an Installation Method menu.

4. Choose Disk Options from the Installation Options menu.

5. Choose Perform Surface Test from the Available Disk Options menu.

6. Check Test Type. Valid entries are: None, the partition is not being tested; Failed, a disk error has occurred; Completed, it tested successfully; Terminated, the test was stopped; Destructive, data will be lost; or Nondestructive, all data will be preserved.

7. Choose Begin Surface Test from Surface Test Options.

8. Choose the type of test (destructive or nondestructive) and begin the test.

DET and FAT tables hold valuable information. Directory Entry
Table (DET) and File Allocation Table (FAT) contain address
information about where data can be retrieved from. Duplicate copies
of DET and FAT are stored elsewhere on the disk. Each time the
server is booted, consistency checks are performed on all four files to
verify that their corresponding files are identical. If you get an error
saying they are not, run VREPAIR.

NetWare writes to the drive in blocks of 4, 8, 16, 32 or 64k size.
NetWare uses two methods to verify that data is not written
to unreadable blocks. The first is read-after-write and the second is
Hot Fix.

Read-after-write reads back what it wrote after the write is done
and then checks against what is still in memory. If the data is the
same, then NetWare goes on to the next command it needs to process. If the data is not the same, NetWare goes to Hot Fix.

Hot Fix involves the original block of data being redirected to a
Hot Fix Redirection area where data can be stored. Hot Fix has a
small portion of the disk's storage space set aside for such an occurrence, and it is always active unless the disk fails. After the operating
system has the address of a defective block, the server will not attempt to store data to that block.

**Replication involves placing a copy of a directory partition on
another server.** To have Directory Services across a network
of servers, replicas of each partition are stored on each of the servers
across the network. They eliminate any single point-of-failure and
provide faster access across a WAN link.

Replication of the directory, however, does not provide fault
tolerance for the file system; only the directory information about
objects is replicated. For file fault tolerance, you have to duplex
or mirror.

Know which servers are prime servers. If all servers but one are
taken down, and you cannot access the one remaining, then it
is not a prime server. Use PARTMGR to copy the prime server
partition onto the remaining server, and you will be able to use it.

There is a difference between duplexing and mirroring. Disk Duplexing is the storing of the same information on separate disks with separate controller channels, whereas Disk Mirroring is the storing of the same information on separate disks on the same controller channel. Duplexing is preferred over mirroring because the likelihood of both channels failing simultaneously is rare.

Duplexing alone doesn't guarantee data protection. Both channels may fail simultaneously, and you can lose all data. Back up regularly.

There is a method to the madness of filename extensions. For the most part, NetWare has tried to emulate the extensions used in DOS, and the following are reflective of that use:

BAT	Executable batch file
COM	Executable command file
DAT	ASCII text file
ERR	Error log file
EXE	Executable file
HLP	Help screens
MSG	Message file
OVL	Graphical overlay
SYS	System operating file

The following extensions have no equals in DOS and are NetWare-specific:

DSK	Server disk driver
LAN	Server LAN driver
NAM	NetWare name space support
NCF	NetWare server executable batch file
NDS	NetWare Directory Services file
NLM	NetWare Loadable Module
PDF	Printer definition file
Q	Print job file
QDR	Print queue definition directory

 You can separate power disturbances into three different categories:

- *Transient*. A spike or surge of short duration but extreme in size.

- *Noise or static*. Small changes in voltage.

- *Blackouts and brownouts*. A loss of electricity altogether, or drop in electricity.

Three types of protection against power disturbances are available:

- *Suppression* protects against transients.

- *Isolation* protects against noise using transformers.

- *Regulation* provides Uninterruptible Power Supplies to get through the black- and brownouts.

 There are two types of UPSs:

- Online UPSs actively monitor power going to the unit. Of the two, this type is the more expensive.

- Offline UPSs monitor the power line and come on when they are needed, with a slight lag time—usually only a few milliseconds.

Remember: a UPS saves the server and the files that are open on it, but what about workstations and the data they're holding in their RAM? This information is lost when the workstation power is lost. To ensure complete power security for the network, you must also provide backup power for the workstations.

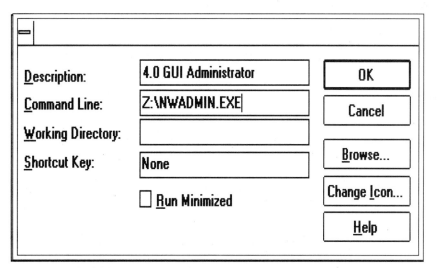

Figure 10-1: SYSCON does not exist in NetWare 4.0. You should access login scripts through NWADMIN or NETADMIN.

If your login scripts do not perform all functions after an up-grade to 4.0, check to see if they contain any of the following commands. If they do, you must modify the scripts after the upgrade.

- *MEMBER_OF_GROUP*. Groups have been replaced by group objects, and this variable is no longer supported.

- *MAP*. When you map a drive to a directory that is located on the Directory Services volume, you do not include the server name in the MAP command; however, when you map a drive to a server that is running a previous version of NetWare, you must leave MAP as it originally appeared.

- *ATTACH*. This command is no longer supported.

If login scripts fail to complete execution, check the order of processing. If the login script executes partially, and it has nothing to do with the upgrade, check to see whether an IF...THEN statement must be satisfied for processing to continue or whether an Exit command precedes further processing.

 If a printer is not working, take it off the network and test it. If it works fine alone, it should work fine on the network, and you now know that the problem is something other than the printer.

If you cannot get a workstation printer to print, make sure the following line is not in NET.CFG:

```
LOCAL PRINTERS=0
```

If this line is in the file, delete it or make the number equal to 1 or the number of printers you have.

 If you're trying to print but nothing prints out, try following these steps:

1. Verify that CAPTURE is active, and was before you tried to print or started the application. You can verify this at the command line by typing **CAPTURE Sh**.

2. Verify that all LPT ports are captured.

3. Go into PCONSOLE and see whether the job is spooling anywhere.

 Corruption can strike any part of the printer objects. If you have corrupted print jobs, unknown queue errors, errors when trying to access a queue or a prompt for a password when the print server is loaded, then delete print queues and print servers and add them again. Their descriptions have become corrupted, and reinstalling the print servers is the only way to truly get rid of all traces of the corruption.

 If a workstation cannot communicate on the network, follow these steps:

1. Check to see that the NIC board is properly seated.

2. Try another board in the workstation and see if it works.

3. Check to see if board settings match the values displayed when you're loading the LAN drivers.

4. Check interrupt settings to see if there is a conflict with other devices. If a modem is in the workstation, pull it out and see if that makes a difference.

5. Check to see if the cable is properly connected and terminated. Is it exceeding the maximum length for the topology? Is this workstation the farthest from the server?

 If a user has trouble logging in and out, follow these steps:

1. Check to see if the password is expired.

2. Verify that the user is on the login drive, F:.

3. If you can you log in from another workstation, check the network card and cabling.

4. Run SLIST to see if the server is up or down.

5. Verify that LOGIN.EXE is in existence and not deleted.

6. Check time restrictions to see if they apply.

 If a workstation screen is frozen, follow these steps:

1. Press Ctrl-Enter to see if a message has come in from another user and needs to be cleared.

2. Try to clear the connection from the server console using the CLEAR utility.

3. Check that cables have not been pulled from the NIC card.

4. Press Ctrl-Alt-Del and try to log back in.

 Protocol analyzers can save troubleshooting time. Protocol analyzers usually cost between $1,000 and $3,000 and provide detailed data on the types of network packets traveling across a LAN for troubleshooting purposes. Filters sift through traffic for particular results, and alarms alert you when predefined thresholds have been exceeded.

Watch for and delete unnecessary directories. If bindery emulation is on, and a user logs in via bindery mode, then a mail directory is created for that user on the filer server running bindery emulation.

A typical CONFIG.SYS file for a workstation looks like the following:

```
files=60
buffers=40
stacks 9,256
lastdrive=z
(for windows - device=c:\windows\himem.sys)
```

A typical AUTOEXEC.BAT file for a workstation looks like the following:

```
c:\windows\smartdrv.exe
@echo off
set temp=c:\windows\temp
prompt $p$g
```

 Following is a typical NET.CFG file, reflecting a NE2000 network card:

```
Link Driver 3C509
  PORT 300
  FRAME Ethernet_802.3
  INT 10

Link Support
  MAX STACKS 8
  BUFFERS 8 1514
  MEMPOOL 4096

SHOW DOTS ON
FILE HANDLES 60

NetWare DOS Requester
  CACHE BUFFERS = 5
  BUFFER SIZE = 1024
  USE DEFAULTS = ON
  VLM = CONN.VLM
  VLM = IPXNCP.VLM
  VLM = TRAN.VLM
  VLM = BIND.VLM
  VLM = AUTO.VLM
  VLM = RSA.VLM
  VLM = NWP.VLM
  VLM = FIO.VLM
  VLM = GENERAL.VLM
  VLM = REDIR.VLM
  VLM = PRINT.VLM
  VLM = NETX.VLM
  CONNECTIONS = 8
  MESSAGE LEVEL = 2
  FIRST NETWORK DRIVE = F
  PREFERRED SERVER ANDERSON
```

```
SIGNATURE LEVEL = 0
NETWORK PRINTERS = 3
SEARCH MODE = 5
LARGE INTERNET PACKETS = OFF
CHECKSUM = 0
```

AUTO.VLM and RSA.VLM work together. You must load both if you want the capabilities they offer enabled. AUTO keeps track of who you are and has the capability to reconnect the workstation automatically if the connection to the server gets lost. RSA rebuilds the authentication, or login, capability.

There is a "watchdog" period for the server, usually of 15 minutes. If connections are broken and reestablished within the watchdog period, the connection is not technically terminated. Upon retry, the connection that did exist will still be in place.

If connections are broken and reestablished outside the watchdog period, the connection is terminated by the watchdog. On retry, AUTO.VLM detects the loss of connection and rebuilds the connection completely. If the server is turned off, whether it is downed or not and then brought back up, the connection is terminated by the shutdown. This situation is the same as a broken connection exceeding the watchdog time limit.

In other words, AUTO and RSA work together to rebuild connections that are inadvertently terminated for less than the time of the watchdog period.

COMMON ERROR MESSAGES

Following is a list of common 4.0 network-related errors, and, when possible, what caused them and how you can rectify the situation.

AUDITCON

- *The auditing system cannot be accessed*—An error condition exists. Down the server, restart it and try again.

■ *This utility was unable to read the bit map*—The bit map cannot be read. Try restarting AUDITCON. If that does not work, down and restart the server.

FILER

■ *Access has been denied*—You don't have the rights to perform the operation you're attempting. Verify rights and grant them where necessary.

■ *The first extended attribute could not be found*—A file being copied has extended attributes that cannot be identified. Try the operation again.

FLAG

■ *Access is denied*—The file is in use, or you are attempting to change rights to a directory that another user is in. Try again later.

■ *The Search mode is not supported for local files*—You can use Search only on network drives and not those on workstations.

■ *This utility was unable to parse the specified path*—The directory path you gave is invalid. Verify and try again, or use MAP if necessary.

LOGIN

■ *Access to the server has been denied*—You don't have an account, or it has been disabled. Try again, verifying the correct login and password.

■ *Access to the server has been denied and you have been logged out*—You were already logged in and tried to do so again. Log in once more.

■ *All drives are in use*—All drives from A to Z are accounted for, and no more can be added. Check where they are being mapped to and remove any that are not appropriate.

- *Insufficient memory is available to add the variable to the path ...*—Not enough room is available in the workstation's environment. Create more room by restarting COMMAND.COM with the "/E" option and specifying more bytes.

- *Intruder detection lockout has disabled this account*—You successfully logged in after exceeding the number of times you could fail. The system administrator has to reenable the login.

- *The line contains no end quote*—A text message has a quotation mark at the beginning of the text but not at the end. Edit the login script, and correct the problem.

- *The line is too long*—A line within your login script is exceeding the 254-character limit. Shorten the line.

- *The NetWare shell is not loaded*—Reboot the workstation and try to log in again.

- *The server does not respond*—Power was lost while files were still open, or the cable has become improperly terminated. Try to isolate the problem.

- *This utility could not get your connection status*—LOGIN was unable to see whether you were already logged in or not. Reboot the workstation, and try to log in again. If this message persists, down the server and restart.

- *This utility was unable to map ...*—The limit of 16 search drives was reached and exceeded. Reduce the number of search drives.

- *You could not be authenticated to server*—The server does not find the login and password you gave. Try again.

MAP

- *Access to the server was denied*—Either your password or login name was given incorrectly. Try logging in again.

- *All drives are in use*—There are no free drives to map. Check the Lastdrive variable to see if it is as low as it can go. If so, begin deleting drives that you don't use on a regular basis.

■ *The server did not respond*—The server is not running, and a DOWN command was not issued, or you have a faulty connection. Check the status of the server.

■ *The specified server is unknown*—The name of the server was either mistyped, or it is not up and running. Type **SLIST** to see a list of valid servers in operation.

NCOPY

■ *Internal error ...*—Try the operation again, verifying syntax. If this error happens again, exit from the subdirectory, and try the operation from one level back.

■ *Multiple files cannot be copied to a single file*—If you're trying to copy and not concatenate, then reissue the command being more specific. If you indeed are trying to concatenate, then use the COPY command from DOS, which does allow you to copy multiple files into one.

■ *The file cannot be copied*—You either have insufficient rights to the file, or it is locked by another user accessing it. Check your rights, and try the operation again when you are certain the file is not in use.

■ *The maximum number of directory levels ...*—NCOPY supports only 25 levels. Use another copy routine, or rearrange the directory so it does not have as many levels.

■ *The server has run out of dynamic memory*—Dynamic memory and RAM are one and the same. The ideal solution is to add more RAM, but for now, reboot the server to clear the memory, and try the copy again.

■ *The server is out of directory entries*—Each volume can hold a specific number of files based on the size of the volume. The best solution is to purge deleted files and retry the operation. If this error persists, archive files no longer needed from the volume, and try once more.

■ *The source file cannot be opened*—The file you're trying to copy is read-only, or it's in use by another user. Check the rights, and try to copy again.

■ *Volume does not exist*—Verify that there are no errors in the command you've given. If not, use FILER to verify the volume does exist.

NETADMIN

■ *Insufficient memory ...*—The workstation does not have enough memory. Reboot the workstation and unload any TSRs; then try again. If the workstation still does not work, add more memory to the workstation or use a workstation that presently has more.

■ *One of the values was deleted by another workstation ...*—Someone else is in NETADMIN accessing the same items you are. Exit the program, and go back in later.

■ *The object could not be added ...*—An internal error prevented NETADMIN from carrying out the command. Exit NET-ADMIN, and go back in to try once more.

PSC

■ *An error occurred while getting the connection status. See your network supervisor*—An internal error caused a process to fail. Try again.

■ *PSC is unable to allocate sufficient memory ...*—The workstation lacks enough RAM to complete the request. Reboot the workstation, and remove any TSR programs. If this method does not work, add more memory, or use a workstation that presently has more.

RIGHTS

■ *An error occurred while ...*—Try the operation again.

■ *Open is invalid with 386 server*—You cannot use the Open right on any server running NetWare 3.x.

- *The message file for this utility cannot be found*—The file RIGHTS.MSG is missing, or it isn't in the search paths. Find it and copy it over, or add it to the search paths.

SBACKUP

- *SBACKUP cannot parse path*—The path specified for the log file does not exist. Correct the path to a valid entry.

- *SBACKUP cannot scan the next data set*—The next item to be scanned has rights and attributes that are preventing you from reading, or the file is presently in use.

- *The message buffer is full. Internal error*—The error message that should appear and explain what has happened cannot do so because the entry is longer than will fit in the buffer. Give Novell a call at 1-800-NOVELL.

SETPASS

- *Account for {server} is restricted. Your password was not changed*—The number of grace logins has expired, and now you cannot change the password. The system administrator can still change it using FILER.

- *An unexpected error occurred ...*—Try the operation again after verifying the server is still up and the workstation connected. Reboot the workstation if necessary.

- *The message file for this utility cannot be found*— SETPASS.MSG is missing or is not in the search path. Locate it, and map a drive over.

WHOAMI

- *An error occurred during ...*—Try again.

- *The message file for this utility cannot be found*— WHOAMI.MSG is missing or is not in the search path. Locate it, and map a drive.

■ *This utility was unable to allocate sufficient memory for the Directory Services attribute buffer*—The workstation lacks sufficient RAM. Reboot, and if that approach does not work, add more memory to the workstation.

SUMMARY

NetWare 4.0 is a rapid departure from the way networking has been approached in previous versions of the operating system. Far from being aimed at the casual user, this version is marketed specifically for large networks with multiple servers and hundreds of workstations.

There is no need for small firms to upgrade because the benefits they receive from version 4.0 are not substantial enough to merit the cost. With a small number of servers, partition replication and the different database structure offer no benefit.

Large accounts, on the other hand, will benefit considerably from the new features and should upgrade with all great haste. They will gain all features discussed in this book, primarily the ability to create huge networks with global features.

Appendix A

UPGRADING TO 4.0

In this appendix, you learn whether you can or cannot upgrade to NetWare 4.0. If you can upgrade, use the steps shown here.

THOSE WHO CAN'T UPGRADE

You cannot upgrade a previous version of NetWare to version 4.0 if the previous version you're trying to upgrade is one of the following:

- version 2.0a

- version 3.0

If you're running either of these two versions, you must first upgrade to a later version of the operating system, or you must format the server and start the 4.0 installation from scratch.

UPGRADING TO 4.0

If you're not running a version of NetWare mentioned in the preceding section, you can begin your upgrade now, using the steps in the following sections.

Step 1

The first thing to do when you plan to upgrade to NetWare 4.0 is make duplicate copies of the NetWare disks. Never use the original disks to do an installation because there is too much likelihood that something will happen to them, and you will be sadly out of luck—to put it nicely.

Step 2

With step 1 accomplished, do a full system backup of the server. If the installation fails halfway through, some files may remain open. If you have to go back to the previous level, restoring from a complete backup is easier than picking your way through a minefield trying to determine what was affected by the upgrade and what was not.

Step 3

If you're running version 3.11, jump to step 5. The Install program works only with version 3.11. If you're running one of the following versions, however, then worry not:

- 2.10
- 2.11
- 2.12
- 2.15(a, b or c)
- 2.2

The upgrade disk contains a version 3.11 SERVER.EXE file, which will make the server a one-user system—enough to get the upgrade going. Bear in mind, however, that you will need enough space to hold the version 3.11 file—approximately 10 percent more than the version 2.1x file.

Start the migration utility. Four things happen while it is running:

1. The version 2.1x system is analyzed and inventoried.

2. The version 2.1x disk is analyzed, and locations for Hot Fix and the FAT are determined.

3. The version 2.1x disk is modified; blocks are moved to new locations.

4. A version 3.11 bindery is created to replace the version 2.1x bindery, and passwords are lost. If you create new passwords for existing users, they are stored in NEW.PWD in the SYS:SYSTEM directory.

Additionally, all information about VAPs (Value Added Processes) is lost because there is no such equivalency in version 3.x. Core printing services are not upgraded, and you must delete any printing services that existed and re-create them entirely. Volume/disk restrictions for users are not carried over because of the differences in the file systems.

Step 4

Make another backup of the server now that it's running version 3.11. This way, you know the conversion is working properly so far, and should you have to go back a few steps and start over, having a backup prevents you from having to go back to the beginning.

Step 5

Run the upgrade utility. It goes through the data on the server and upgrades the following items:

- Bindery objects become directory objects.

- Login scripts are converted as property of the users they are assigned to.

- Netware Directory Services are created.

Bindery objects get upgraded to directory objects in the following manner:

- Group EVERYONE becomes CN=EVERYONE, object class=group.

- Other groups become CN=group_name, object class=group.

- User GUEST becomes CN=GUEST, object class=user.

- User SUPERVISOR becomes CN=SUPERVISOR, object class=user.

Watch for identical names. If you upgrade several servers into the same context, and several users with identical names appear in context, the login script of the first user that was upgraded takes precedence over subsequent login scripts of other users with the same name.

Be wary of the C container. The C= country container is not implied during installation and there are good reasons not to use this optional feature. When you use it, you must explicitly type out the full name anytime you are addressing an object for broadcasting or sending messages.

Appendix B

SETTING PARAMETERS

Following is a listing of the most-often configured parameters that you can set in the .NCF files, as well as their default settings and allowable values. For a complete listing, see the electronic text supplied with the operating system.

Communications	default	values
Console display watchdog logouts	Off	On, off
Delay before first watchdog packet	5 min.	15 sec.–20 min.
Delay between watchdog packets	59 sec.	1 sec.– 0 min.
Maximum packet receive buffers	100	50–2000

Maximum physical receive packet size	1130	618–4202
Minimum packet receive buffers	10	10–1000
New packet receive buffer wait time	0.1 sec.	0.1–20 sec.
Number of watchdog packets	10	5–100

Directory Caching	default	values
Dir cache allocation wait time	2 sec.	0.5 sec.–2 min.
Dir cache buffer nonreferenced delay	5 sec.	1 sec.–5 min.
Dirty dir cache time delay	0.5 sec.	0–10 sec.
Maximum dir cache buffers	500	20–4000
Maximum concurrent dir cache writes	10	5–50
Minimum dir cache buffers	20	10–2000

Disk	default	values
Enable disk read after write verify	On	On, off
Remirror block size	1	1–8
Concurrent remirror requests	4	2–32

File Caching	default	values
Dirty disk cache delay time	3 sec.	0.1–10 sec.
Maximum concurrent disk cache writes	50	10–100
Minimum file cache buffers	20	20–1000
Minimum file cache report threshold	20	0–1000
Reserved buffers below 16mb	16	8–200

File System	default	values
Allow deletion of active directories	On	On, off
Compression daily check stop hour	6	0–23

Compression daily check start hour	0	0–23
Days untouched before compression	5	1–100000
Deleted file compression option	1	0–2
Enable file compression	On	On, off
File delete wait time	5 min.	0 sec.–7 days
Immediate purge of deleted files	Off	On, off
Maximum concurrent compressions	4	1–8
Maximum extended attributes per file	8	4–51
Maximum % of volume per directory	13	5–50
Maximum % of volume space for attributes	10	5–50
Maximum subdirectory tree depth	25	10–100
Minimum compression % gain	5	0–50
Minimum file delete wait time	1 min.	0 sec.–7 days

Single access leave file compressed	On	On, off
Turbo FAT reuse wait time	5 min.	0.3 sec–66 min.
Volume low warn all users	On	On, off
Volume low warning reset threshold	256	0–100000
Volume low warning threshold	256	0–1000000

Lock	default	values
Maximum file locks	10000	100–100000
Maximum file locks per connection	250	10–1000
Maximum record locks	20000	100–200000
Maximum record locks per connection	500	10–10000

Memory	default	values
Auto register above 16mb	On	On, off
Garbage collection interval	15 min.	1–60 min.

Minimum free memory for garbage collection	8000	1000–1000000
Number of frees for garbage collection	1000	100–10000
Read fault emulation	Off	On, off
Read fault notification	On	On, off
Write fault emulation	Off	On, off
Write fault notification	On	On, off

ABEND ABnormal END; a serious hardware or software problem that stops the server.

Access Control List A list of who can access information about objects. A list exists for each object and contains the trustee assignments and the Inherited Rights Filter.

accounting Tracking resources used on the server and/or network.

adapter See *card*.

address The unique number identifying a device in the network.

ADMIN The one user object created automatically during installation or upgrade of NetWare 4.0. This user has trustee rights to the root directory and can create and manage other objects.

application A software program.

archive To transfer files from the server to another storage device, usually tape, or the place where files are stored.

ARCnet A network protocol commonly used when large distances must be covered.

asynchronous Transmission of varying, uneven lengths, wherein characters are differentiated by the addition of start and stop bits.

attach To establish a connection between the workstation and the server.

attenuation How much of the signal is lost over distance.

attributes Characteristics of a file or directory that dictate what actions can be performed.

audit To check network transactions via the AUDITCON utility, or, similarly, to verify that nothing that should not be taking place is.

AUTOEXEC.BAT A batch file automatically executed on a workstation with every bootup. Commands placed in this file establish the environment for the user.

AUTOEXEC.NCF A file automatically executed on a server with each bootup. Commands placed in this file establish the environment for the server.

backbone A cabling system to which only NetWare servers and routers are attached.

bandwidth The number of simultaneous transmissions a cable can transport, usually measured in hertz or cycles per second. The greater the bandwidth, the more it can carry, and the lower the bandwidth, the fewer it can carry.

banner The first page of a print job, indicating what sent it and what follows.

bindery The NetWare database in all versions up to 4.0, where it was replaced by Directory Services.

bindery emulation NetWare 4.0 talks to servers running other versions by emulating the flat structure of their bindery.

block The smallest amount of space that can be allocated at one time on a NetWare volume. The size is dependent on the size of the drive. Beyond this, suballocation in 4.0 works to utilize remainders of unused blocks.

BNC Connectors used on Thin Ethernet coaxial cable and ARCnet.

bridge A specialized server that you can use to connect LANs of different types. The bridge transmits packets from one segment of the network to another segment, while a router forwards packets between topologies.

broadcast A message sent to all of the users on the network at the same time.

buffer An area of memory, or an area on a server, that temporarily holds data.

burst mode A protocol built on top of IPX that speeds the transfer of multiple file reads and writes from a workstation to the server by eliminating the need to acknowledge each packet. Earlier versions of NetWare used one-request/one-response protocol. Burst reduces network traffic.

bus A topology wherein all workstations and the server are connected to a central cable. See also *daisy chain* and *star*.

cache RAM that temporarily stores files and allows them to be read quickly.

card Network cards, also known as Network Interface Cards or NICs, are the backbone of the network. One card is installed at each workstation and one at the server. All communications between the server and workstation are carried across cables connecting the workstation card to the server card. Every packet that is sent over the network comes into the card in your workstation. The card then decides whether the packet is meant for you. If not, it is discarded; if so, it is processed.

client A single-user workstation connected to the server.

client/server computing An environment where application processing is shared between a client workstation and the server.

coax, or coaxial cable A solid wire surrounded by insulation and wrapped in conductive metal mesh.

cold boot To restore an operating system by turning the power off and back on.

collision A disruption in network transmission caused by two workstations sending information that "collides."

compression The reduction in size of infrequently used files to create more space on the hard drive. You must uncompress files before you can read them.

console The monitor and keyboard used to view the NetWare activity.

container objects Objects that contain other objects. The opposite is leaf object.

context The present environment. For example, within the SYS:SYSTEM directory, SYS:SYSTEM becomes the context of your physical location.

controller channel The logical location of the hard disk hardware.

CMIP Common Management Information Protocol; the proposal from the International Standards Organization defining fault management and configuration, among other things.

CSMA Carrier Sense Multiple Access; a protocol used to avoid collisions.

daisy chain One of three physical topologies for connecting workstations to a file server. A single cable connects to each work-station, and the cables run to the server. See also *bus* and *star*.

database, NetWare Bindery on NetWare versions prior to 4.0, or Directory Services on 4.0. A collection of information relevant to users, groups, volumes and so on.

directory The next level of division below a volume; can contain files and/or be broken into further levels as subdirectories.

Directory Entry Table An index to server files and directories in conjunction with the File Allocation Table, allowing the operating system to use them to locate data quickly.

Directory Services The global database that maintains information about every object allowed on the network; also called NDS.

disable To turn off a NetWare feature, such as DISABLE LOGIN.

disk duplexing The storing of the same information on separate disks with separate controller channels. When the primary system fails, the secondary can take over without interrupting network operations.

disk mirroring The storing of the same information on separate disks on the same controller channel. Similar to duplexing, if the primary drive fails but not the controller card, the secondary can take over without an interruption in network operations.

DMA Direct Memory Access; one method by which NIC cards transfer packets between the CPU and the network.

dynamic memory RAM.

effective rights A combination of trustee assignments in an Access Control List and other trustee assignments, including group and security equivalencies.

enable To turn on a NetWare feature, such as ENABLE LOGIN.

Ethernet A network protocol that runs over thick or thin coax (also known as thinnet), twisted pair or fiber optic cable.

fault An error in transmission.

fault tolerance The use of redundancy to reduce the number of faults.

File Allocation Table An index to disk areas where data is stored; also known as FAT.

gateways Task-specific routers often used to move electronic mail from one LAN to another.

group A cluster of users who have the same permissions regarding an object.

Hot Fix If NetWare fails trying to write the contents of memory to a block, it moves the memory contents to another storage area on the disk set aside for such an occurrence. The address of the bad block is then kept in memory and not used further.

hub A wiring block that modifies transmission signals and allows the network to be lengthened or expanded to additional workstations; generally used in star topology.

impedance The amount of resistance, in ohms, the cable is providing to the transmission it is carrying.

Inherited Rights Filter A filter that prevents rights from passing from one object to another when trustee assignments are granted to an object.

internetwork Two or more networks connected by a router.

interrupt A signal to suspend a program temporarily while another job takes over and then return processing back to where it left off.

IPX Internetwork Packet eXchange; a protocol that sends packets to requested destinations on the network. NETX.EXE prepares packets in a network-understandable form before passing them to IPX.

leaf object The lowest level object, for example, the user, printer, etc. Unlike a container object, a leaf object can contain no other objects.

loadable module A program that you can load and unload from server memory while the server is running.

map object The search path that you use to locate an executable file in a directory other than the one you are in; particularly useful with login scripts to set default maps.

MAU Multistation Access Unit.

mb One megabyte is 1,048,576 bytes of storage space.

Media Access Control The rules that LANs utilize to avoid data collisions. These rules may be the type used in token ring or CSMA (Carrier Sense Multiple Access).

multitasking The capability to switch from one application to another without affecting what is transpiring in the first.

NDS See *Directory Services.*

Netwire Novell's online information service, which provides access to NetWare support and information.

NETX.EXE The NetWare shell program that prepares packets in a network-understandable form before passing them to IPX.

NIC See *cards.*

NLM NetWare Loadable Module; loadable utilities that perform functions specific to NetWare. An NLM runs on the same machine as a server or router alongside the operating system. Many of the compiled routines are packaged with NetWare, but you can write others using a compiler, linker and debugger.

node address The unique number that identifies a network board on a network via a node number. Every station must contain at least one unique node number to distinguish it from the rest.

NOS Network Operating System.

objects Network items or resources that you can use to describe anything within the environment, including servers, drives, users, files and so on. There are two key types of objects: container objects and leaf objects. Container objects hold other objects in the way subdirectories hold files. Leaf objects contain no other objects and are users, printers, etc.

object rights One of four types of rights that control what a trustee can do with the object.

ODI Open Data line Interface; an architecture that allows multiple LAN drivers and protocols to exist on the same network.

optical disk A form of removable media used to store data.

Organization object A container below the Country object (if used).

Organizational Role object A leaf object that defines a position or role that different people can fill within an organization.

Organizational Unit object A container object below the Organization level, which differentiates between divisions, departments, teams and so on.

packet A unit of information used in network communications.

packet burst protocol See *burst mode*.

packet switching A method of transmitting individual packets from many users at one time on a single channel.

partitions Logical units into which hard disks are divided. NetWare recognizes DOS and NetWare partitions only; all others are referred to as non-NetWare partitions.

print queue A network directory that stores print jobs.

profile objects Objects containing login scripts that are run by a group of users to give them all the same work environment and drive mappings. An individual user can be a member of only one profile object.

property rights One of the four types of rights existing in NetWare 4.0, with object, directory and file. Property rights control a trustee's access to information stored within the object.

protocol A standardized rule specifying the format of the way information is addressed on the network.

QIC Quarter-Inch Cartridge; a standard format for backup tapes and related devices.

queue An area where information is temporarily stored until it is processed. See also *print queue*.

RAID Redundant Array of Inexpensive Disks; a low-cost series of disks used to increase fault tolerance on a server.

RAM Random Access Memory; memory used to store information that is received or read from a drive or other input device.

read-after-write A verification method wherein NetWare reads back a block of memory that it has just written to and compares it against the original contents still in memory. If the blocks match, processing goes on as normal; otherwise, NetWare utilizes Hot Fix to write the contents elsewhere.

replica A copy of a directory partition. To have Directory Services across a network, replicas of each partition are stored on each of the servers across the network. They eliminate any single point-of-failure and provide faster access across a WAN link.

RIP Router Information Protocol; this protocol tells routers how to exchange information in a NetWare internetwork.

RJ-11 The standard modular telephone connection that supports up to four wires.

RJ-45 Modular telephone-style LAN connectors that hold eight wires.

ROM Read-Only Memory; memory that cannot be written to. Used in diskless workstations to receive the bootup operating system from the server.

root directory The highest level in a hierarchical directory structure.

routers Servers that allow the connection from one LAN to another.

routing Transferring packets from one segment of a network to another.

RS232 The serial interface specification created to outline the method by which data terminals talk to data communication devices.

SCSI Small Computer System Interface; a high-speed data exchange interface that is used mostly with hard drives and tape devices.

search drive A drive letter between A and Z where NetWare looks for an executable file if one matching the command name is not found in the current directory.

server The device shared by all connected workstations. With a file server, files are contained on the hard drive, which all workstations can access. With a print server, all workstations can send documents to this device to be printed.

SLED Single, Large, Expensive Disk; an alternative to RAID that is used for disk mirroring and increasing fault tolerance.

SNMP Simple Network Management Protocol; the suite of protocols developed in conjunction with the U.S. government to define network management.

star One of three physical topologies used in connecting a server to workstations. Each workstation is connected directly to the server or to a wiring hub. See also *bus* and *daisy chain*.

STARTUP.NCF A NetWare server boot file that loads the NetWare server's disk driver.

straight tip Connectors used on fiber optic cables.

synchronous transmission The opposite of asynchronous; all transmissions are of equal length and are not marked by the addition of start and stop bits.

terminator A resistor placed at each end of the network cable to prevent signals from being echoed back down the cable.

time synchronization A method of ensuring that all servers in a directory tree report the same time.

token ring A networking protocol widely recommended by IBM and used in place of ARCnet or Ethernet.

topology The physical layout of a network.

transceiver An electrical component that goes between a workstation and the network backbone wiring; it handles transmissions between the two.

tree A hierarchical structure branching from top to bottom. A directory tree, for example, begins with the directory and then branches to subdirectories and further to files.

trustee A user who has been granted rights to work with a directory, file or object.

TTS Transaction Tracking System; a method of protecting the database from being corrupted by a power failure.

Turbo FAT A special File Allocation Table index used when a file exceeds the block size that still enables the file to be accessed quickly.

user An individual allowed access to the network.

utility In the NetWare sense, a non-essential NetWare application that performs basic tasks.

Virtual Loadable Modules Similar to NLMs, a modular executable program with a set of logically grouped features; also called VLMs. As NLMs operate on the server, VLMs operate on the client.

volume The highest level in the NetWare file system. Created from local partitions, a volume can reside on one or more hard disks.

WAN Wide Area Networks; the antithesis of local area networks, in that their geographic span is over a long distance. Local area networks can become part of a WAN by connecting via a modem or microwave connection.

warm boot To reboot the operating system without removing power from the device; most commonly done on a workstation by pressing the Ctrl-Alt-Del key combination.

wildcard character Any character that stands for another. The most common examples are the asterisk, which stands for anything, and the question mark, which stands for one thing. *.* means all files and all extensions, and ?ET.TXT means only three-letter filenames ending in "ET" and having the extension "TXT."

workstation The personal computer that a user is using to connect to the network.

X.25 A protocol that details packet switching.

COMPANION DISK SNEAK PREVIEW

One of NetWare's more frightening features is its potential for errors. With upwards of 5,000 possible error messages in version 4.0, it's comforting to have a comprehensive resource that relates, in plain English, what happened and why.

Nothing is more frustrating for users or administrators than being confronted with an error on the screen and not knowing what it means or how to handle the problem. With a single error message resource at your fingertips, you can look up the error message and decide how to fix things. The quicker you diagnose the problem, the sooner you can solve it.

The *Voodoo NetWare Companion Disk* features a database of error messages that you can search for details on thousands of specific errors. It tells you the error and also what caused it, as well as the best solution to the problem. No more carting heavy manuals around and flipping through page after page of inscrutable, cryptic messages.

The powerful database on the companion disk is guaranteed to help you respond to problems more quickly, efficiently and decisively. If you're not completely satisfied, your money will be refunded.

INDEX

WORK WONDERS WITH VENTANA VOODOO!

VOODOO DOS, SECOND EDITION
$21.95
277 pages, illustrated
ISBN: 1-56604-046-9
Updated for all versions of DOS through 6.0, *Voodoo Dos, Second Edition*, offers a wide range of time-saving techniques designed for all users. You'll find a wealth of help for customization; using the DOS editor; working with Shell and more! Learn to streamline time-consuming tasks and maximize your DOS productivity!

VOODOO MAC
$21.95
340 pages, illustrated
ISBN: 1-56604-028-0
Whether you're a power user or a beginner, *Voodoo Mac* has something for everyone! Computer veteran Kay Nelson has compiled hundreds of invaluable tips, tricks, hints and shortcuts that simplify your Macintosh tasks and save time, including disk and drive magic, fonta and printing tips, alias alchemy and more!

VOODOO WINDOWS

$19.95
282 pages, illustrated
ISBN: 1-56604-005-1
A unique resource, *Voodoo Windows* bypasses the obtuse technical information found in many Windows books to bring you an abundance of never-before-published tips, tricks and shortcuts for maximum Windows productivity. A one-of-a-kind reference for beginners and experienced users alike.

VOODOO WINDOWS NT

$24.95
385 pages, illustrated
ISBN: 1-56604-069-8
Discover a cauldron of creative advice for mastering Microsoft's powerful new 32-bit operating system! A wealth of techniques for streamlining your work and increasing productivity is at your fingertips with time-saving tips and tricks for a variety of tasks. You'll find hundreds of hints for simplifying your NT tasks without having to wade through obtuse technical information.

VOODOO NETWARE

$27.95
315 pages, illustrated
ISBN: 1-56604-077-9
Overcome network computing obstacles with insightful tips, tricks and shortcuts from *Voodoo NetWare*. This unique guide offers network managers an unparalleled collection of advice for troubleshooting, increasing user productivity and streamlining NetWare tasks. NetWare 4.0 users will find timely tips for a variety of commands and features.

> **Special Offer: Buy all five books in the Ventana Press Voodoo™ Series Library and pay just $81.75, a 30% savings!**

For faster service, order toll-free 800/743-5369.
Ventana Press, P.O. Box 2468, Chapel Hill, NC 27515 (919) 942-0220; Fax: (919) 942-1140

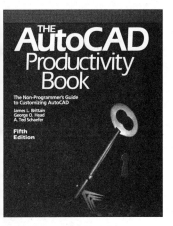

The AutoCAD Productivity Book

The world's most widely used reference on customizing AutoCAD. You'll find step-by-step chapters on simple methods for creating your own dialogue boxes, revising screen and tablet menus, using DOS to customize AutoCAD and much more!

Companion disk:
- 30 productivity-enhancers AutoCAD forgot about, including metric conversion, copy from Paper Space, Break, Merge and Bold text, exploding all polylines and more!

$27.95 for book only
$77.90 for book with diskette
369 pages, illustrated
ISBN: 1-56604-026-4

AutoLISP in Plain English

At last, an AutoLISP reference that anyone can understand! This basic guide introduces you to the tools you'll need to create simple, useful AutoLISP programs that solve everyday drawing tasks.

Companion disk:
- All lesson programs in the first ten chapters.
- 20 "working" programs featured in Chapter 11.
- Plus 7 programs not found in the book!

$23.95 for book only
$43.90 for book with diskette
272 pages, illustrated
ISBN: 1-56604-009-4

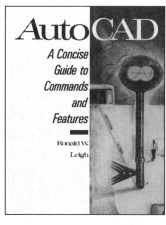

AutoCAD: A Concise Guide to Commands & Features

Completely updated and revised for Release 12, this book offers beginners the most complete, easy-to-read introduction to AutoCAD, including all essential terms and techniques, step-by-step operating instructions on setting up, drawing, editing, saving and more!

Companion disk:
- All drawings and exercises in the book, enabling you to load them without reconstructing them by hand.

$24.95 for book only
$44.90 for book with diskette
447 pages, illustrated
ISBN: 1-56604-008-6

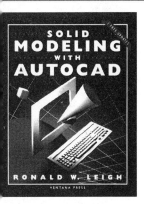

Solid Modeling With AutoCAD

The first book that helps you understand AutoCAD's Advanced Modeling Extension (AME). Completely updated for AME 2.1, you'll learn how to produce realistic-looking 3D drawings, use these drawings to calculate volume, center of gravity and other mass computations. Your one stop guide to AME!

Companion disk:
- Time-saving batch files.
- Pausing scripts.
- 19 AutoLISP programs from Chapter 11.
- Plus 7 programs not found in the book!

$29.95 for book only
$79.90 for book with diskette
327 pages, illustrated
ISBN: 1-56604-004-3

Available through your authorized AutoCAD dealer, bookstores or Ventana Press, P.O. Box 2468, Chapel Hill, NC 27515. 919/942-0220; FAX 919/942-1140. For orders and sales inquiries, call us toll-free at 1-800-743-5369.

VENTANA PRESS

"GETTHREADHANDICAPAMOUNT CALLED WITH INVALID PROCESS ID IN KERNEL."

Inscrutable? Yes! Avoidable? Unlikely! The complexity of NetWare means that error messages are part of the job. So is finding a fast solution.

The *Voodoo NetWare Companion Disk* contains a database of all of the approximately 5000 error messages that can occur in NetWare 4.0, along with causes and likely solutions. No hefty manuals to wade through, no lengthy phone calls to wait out. Just type in the error message and read the answer.

If your job—or your sanity—rely on getting the network back up and running in a minimum of time, this powerful database is an invaluable tool. Satisfaction is guaranteed, or your money returned in full.

TO ORDER additional copies of *Voodoo NetWare* or any other Ventana Press book, please fill out this order form and return it to us for quick shipment. Ask about other books in the Ventana Voodoo™ Series!

	Quantity		Price		Total
Voodoo NetWare	_____	x	$27.95	=	$_____
Voodoo OS/2	_____	x	$24.95	=	$_____
Voodoo Mac	_____	x	$21.95	=	$_____
Voodoo Windows	_____	x	$19.95	=	$_____
Voodoo DOS, 2nd Ed.	_____	x	$21.95	=	$_____
Ventana Voodoo™ Series Library (all 5 Voodoo books)	_____	x	$81.75	=	$_____
Visual Guide to Visual Basic Windows, 2nd Ed.	_____	x	$29.95	=	$_____
The AutoCAD 3D Companion	_____	x	$27.95	=	$_____
The AutoCAD Productivity Book, 5th Ed.	_____	x	$27.95	=	$_____
Solid Modeling With AutoCAD, 2nd Ed.	_____	x	$29.95	=	$_____
AutoLISP in Plain English, 4th Ed.	_____	x	$23.95	=	$_____
1,000 AutoCAD Tips & Tricks, 3rd Ed.	_____	x	$27.95	=	$_____
AutoCAD: A Concise Guide, 3rd Ed.	_____	x	$24.95	=	$_____
Outside AutoCAD	_____	x	$29.95	=	$_____

Shipping: Please add $4.50/first book for standard UPS, $1.35/book thereafter; $8.25/book UPS "two-day air," $2.25/book thereafter. For Canada, add $6.50/book. $_____

Send C.O.D. (add $4.50 to shipping charges) $_____
North Carolina residents add 6% sales tax $_____

Total $_____

Name _____ Co. _____

Address (No PO Box) _____

City _____ State _____ Zip _____

Daytime telephone _____

____ VISA ____ MC Acc't # _____

Exp. Date _____ Interbank # _____

Signature _____

Please mail or fax to: Ventana Press, PO Box 2468, Chapel Hill, NC 27515
919/942-0220 FAX: 919/942-1140
CAN'T WAIT? CALL TOLL FREE: 800/743-5369